THE GREEKS

ALSO BY PAUL CARTLEDGE

Democritus (Great Philosophers Series)

The Cambridge Illustrated History of Ancient Greece

Kosmos: Essays in Order, Conflict, and Community in Classical Athens

The Greeks: A Portrait of Self and Others

THE GREEKS

CRUCIBLE OF CIVILIZATION

Paul Cartledge

New York

LIBRARY OF CONGRESS CATALOGING-IN-PUBLICATION DATA
available on request from the publisher.

ISBN 1-57500-093-8

Art credits can be found on page 254.

The publisher has made every effort to secure permission
to reproduce copyrighted material and would like to
apologize should there have been any errors or omissions.

TV BOOKS, L.L.C.
1619 Broadway, Ninth Floor
New York, NY 10019
www.tvbooks.com

Interior design by Rachel Reiss
Manufactured in the United States of America

CONTENTS

Acknowledgments

Atlantic TV Productions, through Anthony Geffen and Cassian Harrison, first hired me as consultant to the PBS TV series they were preparing entitled "The Greeks." This collaboration I found both very enjoyable and very illuminating, so the idea of a book to accompany the series (not a book "of" the series) that arose during the course of research and filming was welcome. Through the good offices of Robert Gwyn Palmer, an agreement was reached with TV Books, where Keith Hollaman and Albert DePetrillo have proved most congenial editors. My friend, colleague and former pupil Lene Rubinstein generously and with her usual acuity commented on a draft of the entire text. But I, of course, am entirely responsible for the text that follows, and for any remaining errors or infelicities that it may contain.

LIST OF ILLUSTRATIONS AND MAPS

INSERT:

Time Line

(All dates are B.C.E. unless otherwise stated; many are approximate, especially those pre-500)

700	Homer
650–600	Sappho
570	Birth of Cleisthenes
522 (–486)	Darius I of Persia
508	Democracy at Athens
?505	Death of Cleisthenes
499 (–494)	Ionian Revolt
?493	Birth of Pericles
490	Battle of Marathon
486 (–465)	Xerxes of Persia
484	Birth of Herodotus
480	Invasion of Xerxes: Battle of Salamis
479	Battle of Plataea
478	Delian League formed
472	Performance of Aeschylus's *Persians*
469	Birth of Socrates
462/1	Democratic Reforms of Ephialtes and Pericles
460 (–445)	First Peloponnesian War
?460	Birth of Thucydides
447 (–432)	Building of the Parthenon
440–439	Revolt of Samos
?440	Birth of Cynisca
?	Diotima foretells and averts Great Plague of Athens
	Arrival in Athens of Pasion

431 (–404)	Peloponnesian War
?425	Publication of Herodotus's *Histories*
?420	Birth of Epaminondas
404–3	Thirty Tyrants at Athens
403	Restoration of Democracy at Athens; General Amnesty
399	Trial and Death of Socrates
395 (–386)	Corinthian War
386	King's Peace
?385	Plato founds Academy
384	Birth of Aristotle
379–8	Liberation of Thebes
378	Re-foundation of Boeotian federal state Foundation of Second Athenian Sea-League
377 (–353)	Mausolus satrap of Caria
371	Battle of Leuctra
362	Battle of Mantinea
359	Accession of Philip II of Macedon
357	Marriage of Olympias to Philip II
356	Birth of Alexander
356 (–346)	Third Sacred War
357 (–355)	Social War
353	Mausoleum constructed at Halicarnassus
338	Battle of Chaeronea
336	Accession of Alexander
?335	Aristotle founds Lyceum
334	Alexander begins Asia campaign
331	Battle of Gaugamela
323	Death of Alexander the Great
323 (–322)	Lamian War
323 (–30)	Hellenistic era
322	Death of Demosthenes and Aristotle Athenian Democracy terminated

316   Death of Olympias
31   Battle of Actium
30   Death of Cleopatra
        tus
        :onstantinople
        inople

NOTE ON PRONUNCIATION

R eaders unfamiliar with ancient Greek, or with modern Greek, may like to be given some idea of how to
pronounce ancient Greek names of persons and places.

Some, of course, are so familiar that we think of them
almost as English, such as Aristotle, which is in fact an
Anglicized form. In Greek, modern (e.g., the given name
of the shipping magnate Aristotle Onassis) as well as ancient, Aristotle is a five-syllable word: A-ri-sto-te-les,
with the stress falling on the penultimate syllable, thus—
Aristote'les. Actually, that name is a combination of two
other words: *ariston*, "best," and *telos*, "end." Many Greek
personal names had meanings in this way.

Sometimes, rather than Anglicizing, we Latinize ancient Greek proper names. Thus, our Achilles (Latin
form) was in its original Greek form Achilleus (the "ch"
stands for the Greek letter *khi*, which was probably pro-
nounced as a guttural sound rather like gargling from the
back of the throat). The Greeks themselves "translated"
foreign names that sounded strange to them. The Persian
king Artaxerxes, for instance, was in Persian something
like "Artakhshayathra." Yet Herodotus was convinced
that all Persian names ended in "s"!

Place names are generally more straightforward.
Rhodes, like Aristotle, is an Anglicized form. The Greek
original in transcription is the disyllabic "Rhodos," which
in its Latinized form becomes Rhodus. Sometimes it is

necessary to distinguish a political from a geographical use of a place name. Thus, Macedon stands for the kingdom of Macedon, whereas Macedonia is a geographical appellation. Philip and Alexander were kings of Macedon, but ruled over much more than just Macedonia.

Finally, some Greek words just cannot be easily or unambiguously translated. For example, the combination of *de'mos* and *kra'tos* yields Greek *demokratia*, which can be transliterated as "democracy." But the Greek *demos*, though usually translated as "People," does not mean "People" in any sense with which we are familiar, so here it has usually been left in its original form and printed in italics to remind us of its peculiarity.

INTRODUCING THE GREEKS

PRIAM PLEADING WITH ACHILLES FOR THE BODY OF HECTOR
Gavin Hamilton, 1775

The painter has depicted the climactic moment of the *Iliad*, the world's first literary masterpiece, when the Anger of Achilles is at last softened. "Achilles," pleads the aged king of defeated Troy, "show reverence to the mighty gods, and have pity on me—remembering your own father." Priam's plea was answered: leonine Achilles "took the old man's right hand by the wrist and held it, to allay his fears," and then at last returned the corpse of Hector to his father for due burial. *(Tate Gallery, London)*

In any careful study of the lives and times of the ancient Greeks two points become abundantly clear. The first is that they are so like us in so many fundamental ways. The second is precisely the opposite: that they are so *unlike* us in so many fundamental ways. It is as an attempt to embrace both sides of the equation with equal firmness that this new biographically-slanted account is offered and should be judged.

Consider, as a first test case, our English language of politics. The word "language" itself we take from the Romans, in silent acknowledgment of the Roman empire's massive impact—truly a thousand-year Reich—and outreach. But the alphabet we use to write that language is, like the word "alphabet" itself, originally Greek. That it was transmitted to us by the Romans is one of the nicest illustrations of their key role in mediating our Hellenic or ancient Greek heritage. Few clearer examples of our deep debt to that heritage present themselves than the whole sphere of politics. Not only is the word itself ancient Greek in origin, but it carries with it such everyday political terms as "democracy" (People-power, literally) and, at the opposite extreme, "monarchy" (rule by a single individual) and "tyranny" (rule by an unaccountable, non-legitimate despot).

Yet our modern, Western ideas of democracy and monarchy are actually quite different from those of the ancient Greeks. What we call democracy, a system under which we hand over the direction of public affairs to a few representatives who are rarely subject to our immediate control, the ancient Greeks would regard as oligarchy—yet another Greek-derived political word meaning the rule of a few. What we call monarchy, they would not have recognized as a legitimate and meaningful form of political rule at all. Identity of vocabulary can both indicate a shared cultural inheritance and disguise a deep cultural gulf.

There lies one of the perennial fascinations of studying the ancient Greeks, and especially their politics, within the wider context of their culture and society. Whereas we mostly think of politics today as happening in a specific, rather remote place—the Houses of Parliament or Congress—the Greeks saw politics everywhere and saw everything as having a political dimension. It was politics that gave shape, structure, and meaning to all aspects of their everyday lives. They even identified themselves as "political animals," in Aristotle's famous phrase from the first book of his *Politics* (composed in the 330s B.C.E.).

The Greek word from which all these ancient and modern uses of "political" are ultimately derived is *polis*, which is usually translated as either "city-state" or just "city." In all, there were well over a thousand of these, perhaps as many as fifteen hundred, scattered from the eastern end of the Black Sea (in what is now Georgia) to the southern and eastern coasts of Spain at the western end of the Mediterranean. They ranged in territorial size from Sparta in the Peloponnese of mainland Greece (eight thousand square kilometers, three thousand square miles) through Syracuse in Sicily (four

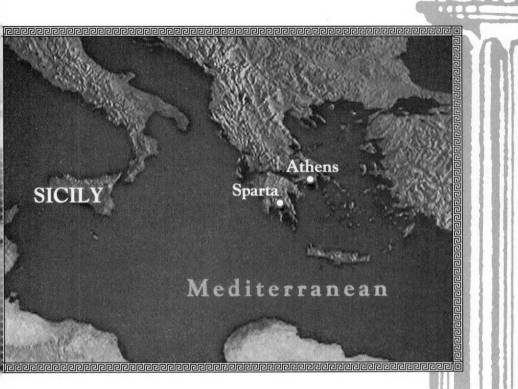

The Central and Eastern Mediterranean, showing the locations of the two most important cities of Classical Greece, Sparta and Athens. It was Athens' lust for the conquest of Sicily that most harmed its cause in the Peloponnesian War (431–404) against Sparta.

THE ERECHTHEUM

The female figures taking the place of columns are called Caryatids. The Caryatid porch shown here is the most familiar view of the temple on the Athenian Acropolis dedicated to Athena and Poseidon but known as the Erechtheum after Erechtheus, the mythical founding king of Athens. Lord Elgin succeeded in removing a Caryatid to London; the remainder of the originals have had to be removed to the safety of an enclosed museum to avoid further pollution damage.

thousand square kilometers), and Athens (twenty-five hundred) down to Corinth (ninety) and even smaller states. Their populations typically numbered only a few thousand, though that of Athens may have reached a quarter of a million at its peak in the late fifth century B.C.E. They governed themselves in a wide variety of ways, but although by no means all of them were always, or ever, democratic, the important thing was that they governed themselves.

The essential criteria of a community's counting as a true *polis* were that it was not ruled directly by a foreign power, even another Greek one, and that it chose its own mode of self-government. However, for military purposes above all, the principles of independence and autonomy were not incompatible in practice with membership in a multi-state alliance such as the Peloponnesian League headed by Sparta, or even in a federal "superstate" such as Boeotia (headed by Thebes). Sometimes these principles were honored more in the breach than the observance. For conspicuous instance, the fifth-century empire of the Athenians represented a notable infringement of *polis* autonomy, notwithstanding all its counterbalancing positive virtues.

Within any one Greek city by no means were all Greeks rated equal—that is, equally meriting full enjoyment of the city's political privileges. Apart from the under-age and the foreign and of course the unfree, who were debarred from virtually all of the citizens' entitlements by definition, adult women too were excluded from many of them by reason of their gender. In an important sense the Greek city was a sort of men's club, even if the high wall erected in theory between men and their mothers, sisters, wives, and daughters might sometimes be scaled or even quite radically undermined.

Despite an obviously diverse political and cultural landscape, the majority of the inhabitants of ancient Greece did share a common cultural bond. This common Hellenic culture was expressed most vividly through religion. As they met each other, or competed against each other, at one of the great pan-hellenic ("All-Greek") religious festivals such as the Olympic Games, they were doing at least three things: competing for personal glory (or watching the contests), worshipping their gods, and—not least—celebrating their common Greek identity. At Delphi, the supposed navel of the ancient Greek universe, the oracle of Apollo speaking through the mouthpiece of his priestess provided an alternative focus for this shared heritage. The great fifth-century historian Herodotus summed it up in a sentence, as only a connoisseur and advocate of pan-hellenic identity could: common language (if with different dialects), common customs and mores (especially religious), and common "blood" (shared descent both in historical reality and in commonly accepted myths of origin). These three components went to make up "the fact of being Greek."

Such Hellenism or Greekness by no means always caused Greeks to automatically pull together in common causes, even in crises; in fact, it all too rarely did that, because of the Greeks' fierce attachment to their primary political *polis*-identity. But it was always there in the background and it did crucially help them to define their ethnic identity. As often as not, this was done by way of distinction from, or outright opposition to, all non-Greeks. These they labeled collectively, and often derogatorily, as "barbarians," originally so called because they were speakers of unintelligible, "bar-bar"-sounding languages.

This Greek-Barbarian opposition is present in Homer, the Greeks'—and the Western world's—first major literature, but it is not especially marked there nor is it entirely negative. Two or three centuries later, however, in the time of Herodotus, it had become firmly established, culturally foun-

HERODOTUS

This imaginary representation of the "father of history," as Cicero called him, does justice to Herodotus's extraordinary vision and pioneering achievement: "This," he wrote in his Preface, "is the exposition of the enquiries of Herodotus of Halicarnassus, carried out so as to ensure that the great deeds of both Greeks and non-Greeks do not lack their due share of fame and, especially, to explain why they fought against one another." *(Museo Nazionale, Naples)*

ITALY

GREECE

PERSIAN EMPIRE

Mediterranean

EGYPT

Central and Eastern Mediterranean, showing the location of the core Greek world between the age-old civilization of Egypt to the south and the Persian Empire to the West. Greeks emigrated from the Aegean core, beginning in the eleventh century B.C.E., and by the time of the Persian invasions in the early fifth century there were Greek communities scattered "like frogs around a pond" (as Plato put it) from one end of the Mediterranean basin to the other and around the Black Sea to the north-east.

dational, and predominantly pejorative. Two historical factors were chiefly responsible for this sea-change in "national" self-consciousness.

First, there were the movement and settlement of Greeks away from the original Aegean heartland, to occupy most shores of the Mediterranean and Black Seas between about 750 and 500 B.C.E. This movement is usually referred to as "colonization," but actually the new Greek foundations were from the start independent cities, not colonies as we understand that term today. Settlers had been attracted or driven to such foundations as Syracuse in Sicily and Olbia on the north shore of the Black Sea by a mixture of motives and conditions—poverty, greed, adventurism, a sense of religious destiny.

In some areas Greek settlers found themselves in contention with settlers of other nationalities, as for example with Phoenicians (from modern Lebanon) on Sicily and Cyprus. Sometimes, relations with the indigenous populations were good from the start, as at Megara Hyblaea in eastern Sicily and Massalia (modern Marseilles); usually they were bad at the start but improved. Sometimes, unfortunately, as at Taras (Taranto in the instep of Italy), they were bad from start to finish. In all cases these relations helped to define by opposition what it meant to be Greek, and colonial Greeks were soon to be found taking a prominent part in the panhellenic festivals celebrated back in the old country.

The second major factor in defining Greekness by negative opposition to barbarians was the attempt by a large number of barbarians—the Persians and their assorted imperial subjects—to conquer mainland Greece in the first two decades of the fifth century. In fact, a number of Greeks living on the Asiatic mainland or on Cyprus had been conquered by and incorporated into the Persian Empire as early as the 540s. Most of these had risen up in revolt in 499 but the revolts were crushed half a dozen years later. It was mainly Athens' involvement in this rising that led to the first of the two major Persian invasions of mainland Greece. This chiefly punitive seaborne expedition ordered by King Darius in 490 ended in the Athenians' remarkable victory at Marathon. The second invasion was a much larger expedition of both revenge and intended conquest, actually led in person by Darius' son Xerxes in 480. The impact of this on Greek identity was complex and decisive. Thereafter the barbarian negative stereotype, visible soon after in Aeschylus's tragedy *Persians* (472) and later in more subtle form in Herodotus's *Histories*, dominated Greek consciousness.

It also provided the psychological and spiritual underpinning of the next wave of Greek permanent emigration, launched by and following in the wake of the astonishing conquests of Alexander the Great (reigned 336 to 323). As a result Greeks and Greek culture penetrated the entire Middle East and extended their reach as far afield as central Asia in the northeast and Pakistan and India in the southeast. The consequences are still visible and palpable today—for example, in the beatification of Alexander within the Coptic Christian church of Egypt and his appearance in some seventy national literatures.

Alexander's empire and, of course, imperialism served as the main cultural bridge between West and East in antiquity. The so-called Hellenistic period (c. 323–30 B.C.E.) ensued, during which much of this new Greek world fell under the sway of a new Western empire, that of Rome. It ended with the defeat in 31 B.C.E. of Antony and Cleopatra at Actium in northwest Greece by the first Roman emperor, Augustus.

In a sense, ancient Hellenism lived on through the Byzantine world founded by Christian emperor Constantine in the fourth century of our era, until that world, too, was brought to an end finally by the Ottoman Turkish conquest of Constantinople in 1453. Scholars fleeing from the fall of Byzantium contributed vitally to the Italian Renaissance, through which the heritage of Hellenism was channeled to our own day.

THIS TENSION OF SAMENESS AND difference that strikes anyone examining the political life of the ancient Greeks is further evident in their culture, society, and economy.

The English poet Philip Larkin humorously claimed that sexual intercourse had been invented in 1963. The Greeks, who brought us "pornography" (meaning, literally, writing about or depicting prostitutes), would not have been slow to dispute that. Their ways of having sex are, of course, as much a defining part of their cultural identity as they are of any other people's. But in one respect, homosexuality, their sexual mores and practices have a further claim to fame and our attention. Highly contested and deeply controversial though it may be, Greek (male) homosexuality is the ultimate fount and origin of an important modern social practice and identity.

It is not so long ago that "Greek love" was a euphemism for what has become known as gay sexuality, and "lesbian" pays silent tribute to the poetry and life of Sappho of Lesbos, replacing the earlier euphemistic term "Sapphic." But it is worth recalling that homosexuality, the word, is only just over a century old. A "gay" today is not precisely what a "homosexual" was a hundred years ago, and in ancient Greece there were neither gays nor homosexuals as we would understand those terms. To take just three of our featured ancient Greeks: Sappho was probably in fact what we would call bisexual, though she may have passed from a predominantly homoerotic to a chiefly heterosexual (married) lifestyle. Socrates too got married, indeed was possibly married to two women simultaneously, but he did nothing to repress his strong homosexual proclivities, even if he seems not to have indulged them physically. Alexander, finally, seems to have married—again, twice—only for dynastic reasons; he was apparently a preferred homosexual. Similarity and difference, therefore, once again.

IF ANCIENT GREEK HOMOSEXUALITY in some respects at least can plausibly be claimed as a cultural ancestor, that cannot easily be argued for ancient Greek pre-Christian or pagan religion. The Greeks did not have a single word corresponding to our "religion" (which comes from the Latin). They used instead various paraphrases, most often a formula meaning literally "the things of the gods." The plural, gods, was and is vital. For the Greeks, the whole world was full of a multiplicity of supernatural and superhuman powers, male and female or neuter, sometimes, when thought of in human form, called gods/goddesses, sometimes, when thought of more abstractly, called demons (*daimonia*).

The New Testament mentions some famous demons, especially those cast out by Jesus's miracle-working. But though written in (Hellenistic) Greek, the New Testament bears witness to a religion radically different from Greek paganism. It was a book, or series of books, composed by and for Hellenized Jews living in the eastern, Greek-speaking half of the Roman empire. Its main aim was to spread the new, Pauline gospel of the risen Christ (that Greek word translates the Hebrew "Messiah," meaning "the Anointed"). A skeptic might want to see more than a trace of pre-Christian polytheism lingering in the later Christian doctrine of the Trinity, not to mention the cult of many saints. But in principle Christianity (like its parent, post-Exilic Judaism) was a strict monotheism, which believed not only that there was only one true God but also that God had singlehandedly created the universe and all that therein moved.

Pagan Greeks—that's what "Hellenes" means in the New Testament—believed quite the opposite. Instead of one, there existed many gods and goddesses, and the universe predated them and had given birth to them, not vice versa. The Greeks' loose and heterogeneous stock of creation myths went with an absence of dogma, a lack of sacred scriptures, and the nonexistence of a privileged vocational priesthood uniquely authorized to interpret them for the laity (from Greek *laos*, "people"). On the whole cult-practices and rituals—what one did—mattered more for pre-Christian Greeks than did faith—what one believed and thought. In short, although Byzantium played a crucial role in preserving and transmitting pagan Greek literature, the ancient Greek legacy does not extend to religion.

At least, not in a direct and immediate sense. Two of our key cultural assets, the theater and competitive athletic sports, do derive ultimately from ancient Greek religious contexts. If the peculiarities and essences of the ancient originals are to be grasped at all accurately, however, the emphasis must fall rather on spiritual difference and cultural unfamiliarity than on what ancient and modern theater and athletics have in common. One way of conveying this emphasis is to concentrate on the central sacrificial rituals of the Olympic Games and the annual Great Dionysia play festival at Athens.

Zeus and Dionysus respectively were worshiped most spectacularly through the ritual slaughter of large numbers of beasts, the cooked flesh of which was distributed among the competitors, pilgrims, spectators, and other participants; the gods themselves received only the smell of the offerings burnt on the altars. The animal blood-sacrifice thus symbolized both the inseparable connection and the unbridgeable gap between mortals and immortals.

Not all-ancient Greeks practiced such sacrifice. The Orphics and Pythagoreans set themselves apart as religious sects precisely by refusing to do so. Other Greeks took a naturalistic or even skeptical attitude towards the nature and very existence of the gods. Xenophanes of Colophon (in Asia Minor; he flourished c. 550 B.C.E.) famously said that if horses and cattle had hands and could draw, they would draw their gods in the form of horses and cattle, and he observed that the non-Greek Thracians depicted their gods as having red hair and blue eyes just like themselves. By implication, the Greeks' own anthropomorphic representations of the divine were no less culturebound. A century after Xenophanes, the famous teacher Protagoras, from Abdera in northern Greece, denied that he could know for sure whether the gods existed, or of what form they were made, since the subject was an obscure one and human life was short. Out of such critical theological speculation was Greek philosophy born.

THE ACTIVITY OF PHILOSOPHIZING in ancient Greece was recognizably ancestral to what philosophers do today; the same sorts of issues were tackled in the same sorts of verbal ways, at any rate by many of the ancients. The mathematician A.N. Whitehead may have exaggerated a little when he wrote some years ago that Western philosophy is little more than a series of footnotes to Plato, but a distinguished contemporary philosopher and classicist, Sir Bernard Williams, has pithily remarked in the same vein that the legacy of Greek philosophy to Western philosophy *is* Western philosophy. Looking at ancient Greek philosophy in this way is, of course, to concentrate once again on what we have in common with the Greeks, focusing on and highlighting the rational dimension.

In fact, the Greek achievement in philosophy can be represented within this perspective as the application of humanist, secular rationality to questions (of morality, of existence) that other cultures and traditions have interpreted predominantly or wholly through religious categories of thought. Yet there existed side-by-side other more or less irrational or even anti-rationalist strains of ancient Greek philosophizing, such as the Cynic school. Besides, what counted as a rational or scientific account of phenomena by the ancient Greeks' standards would often no longer pass muster as such with us. In philosophy, as in science, the Greeks were pathbreaking and sometimes breathtakingly original pioneers, but they would probably make rather odd colleagues in the classroom and library or on the lab bench today.

The emergence of philosophizing in sixth- and fifth-century B.C.E. Greece was part of a wider movement sometimes called the Greek Enlightenment. This is on the assumption that it was somehow comparable in attitude, approach, and achievement to the European and American Enlightenments of the eighteenth century. Certainly, that analogy is useful, up to a point. Philosophy, history-writing, higher education, rhetoric, and various branches of science, especially medicine, did acquire their own professional identities and disciplinary codes. They did make what we would want to recognize as major intellectual advances. However, they coexisted with ways of thinking about the past, instructing the rising generations, healing the sick, and more generally forming world pictures of animate and inanimate nature that were firmly traditional.

Besides, the ancient Greeks had a very different attitude from ours to innovation as such. For most Greeks what was new was shocking in a wholly negative sense. For instance, the Greek terms for political revolution were the equivalent of our "innovationism" and "too-new affairs." They had no equivalent at all to our word "progress," and not much that resembled our modern ideas of progress. Only in the sphere of the visual and performing arts was innovation expected and acceptable, although the inseparable connection of those arts to

the worship of the gods ensured more in the way of evolution-
ary continuity than really radical change.

There was a perfectly good reason for all this basic Greek
conservatism. We, through the application of science and
technology, have mastered—and, of course, too often destroyed—a good deal of our natural environment or modified it
to our ends, achieving levels of human productivity via ma-
chines and computers that any pre-scientific or pre-industrial
culture could only dream of. The ancient Greeks, on the other
hand, were largely at the mercy of the brute forces of nature.
Most of them lived at or near the margins of subsistence, all
too liable to being devastated or even wiped out by an untimely crop failure or bout of disease, not to mention the ever-
present threat of destruction through manmade war.

The Greeks, in short, were dominated by, rather than masters of, what we call economic forces. Not surprisingly, economics as we understand it was not one of the branches of
thought or technique significantly developed by them. When
they spoke of *oikonomia*, they meant the prudent management
of an individual private household or estate rather than the
running of a national economy. Even wealthy Greeks, however, could never be confident that they would pass on intact
to their heirs the landed estate they had inherited. As for poor
Greeks, the very idea of transmitting an estate belonged to the
realm of fantasy.

It is this uncompromisingly tough material background that
explains Greek conservatism. It also explains why their pre-
dominant idea of secular change was one of decline, not
progress. Once upon a time, they believed, in a golden age, the
land had flowed automatically with grain, olive oil, and wine,
the Greeks' equivalent of milk and honey. Now, alas, in the age
of iron, things were very much worse, and there was no realistic hope, let alone expectation, that they would or could get

much better in the foreseeable future. Against such a background, the Greeks' intellectual and cultural achievements really do stand out as remarkable.

The Greeks attempted to exploit and transcend that very general idea of irreversible decline by counterposing the new idea of Utopia. (Thomas More's pseudo-Greek coinage means either No-Place or Place of Well-Faring.) The most famous of these imaginary ancient Greek utopias is Plato's *Republic*, an ideal realm ruled wisely by philosopher-kings with a place set aside for everyone and everyone in his or her allotted place, a world of perfect, if rather restricted, justice. Yet even Plato clearly found this academic exercise ultimately unsatisfactory. Philosopher-kings were not exactly thick on the ground in fourth-century Greece. So he spent the last years of his long life (427–347) constructing a far more tightly prescribed New Jerusalem, which he imagined as a brand new Greek city to be founded on the island of Crete. This too failed to convince, at any rate, Plato's most brilliant pupil, Aristotle. He returned to first base as it were, and ended his *Politics* by sketching a "low" or realistic utopia for mortal men rather than demigods to live in.

So we have come full circle back to our starting-point, the law-bound and law-abiding *polis*. This was truly one of the Greeks' greatest collective achievements, and it formed the indispensable framework within which they constructed the legacy of which we are still—or should be—the grateful legatees.

ALL HISTORY IS PRESENT HISTORY in the sense that the concerns of the present are bound somehow to affect the way history is studied and written. All history is also personal, since it is impossible to avoid the influence of one's own opinions and prejudices on the selection and emphasis of one's historical material. The following account, in pretty much chronological sequence, of the lives and times of eight Greek men (including one naturalized Greek) and seven Greek women (including one who was possibly a fictional creation) in alternation, from Homer (who flourished around 700 B.C.E.) to Alexander the Great (who died in 323 B.C.E.), may require therefore some preliminary explanation and justification.

The ancient Greeks themselves wrote androcentric (man-centered), if not male chauvinist, history. They were aware that women were half the human race, but only occasionally did they give due recognition to the significant historical contributions of individual women. We can, and must, do better, by giving ancient Greek women something like parity of esteem and attention. Likewise, the Greek civilization that was created and enjoyed by free Greeks of citizen status was at least partly dependent on the contribution of the many thousands of men and women who were not citizens, including those who were both non-Greek and unfree. At least one of my subjects (Pasion) began his life in the Greek world as a "barbarian" (non-Greek) slave. Another (Neaera) was accused of having been a slave prostitute before she began a second career as an (allegedly) kept whore whom her Athenian-citizen partner illegally passed off as his lawfully wedded wife.

The inclusion of the selected poets (Homer, Sappho) and philosophers (Socrates, Aristotle) requires no further justification here. Men and women of action (Cleisthenes, Artemisia, Pericles, Epaminondas, Olympias, Alexander the Great): they were all people of the greatest distinction and historical significance. The choice of Diotima, who may be entirely a fictional creation, probably needs defending most of all. She is intended not only to represent the important class of Greek women with religious influence but also to stand as a surrogate for her inventor, Plato, who is not given a chapter to himself (partly because he was yet another Athenian, partly because he was so eccentric and atypical in so many ways), but is represented indirectly not only by Diotima but also by his teacher, Socrates, and by his most distinguished pupil, Aristotle.

Clearly, it was not possible in a small compass to include all the "great" (or greatest) ancient Greeks. Some readers may, for example, regret the absence of chapters on the three great Athenian tragedians of the fifth century. One reason for their omission was my wanting to shift the focus, at least to some extent, away from the all too familiar concentration on Athens and especially on Athens in the fifth century. Greek civilization happened in other cities and at other times, too.

Through the lives of these fifteen men and women, therefore, the major themes of literature, visual art, sexuality, politics (especially democratic), relations with non-Greeks, home life, philosophy, war, athletics, federalism, religion, slavery, economics, and cultural influence can and will be presented and explored in an unusually gripping and vivid manner.

These fifteen ancient Greeks, moreover, stand for a culture and a civilization that still mean a great deal to our own in all sorts of different ways, some more openly acknowledged than others. I hope that my treatment of them will adequately reflect the current ferment of research and controversy in a field, Classics, that is still very much alive and kicking despite its pre-eminent concern with the long dead.

CHAPTER 1

HOMER
OF CHIOS

Apotheosis of Homer

Jean Auguste Dominic Ingres

So great was Homer's reputation that in antiquity it was imagined that after his death he must have been raised to be among the immortal gods. An ancient depiction of this apotheosis in the form of a marble relief datable to about 200 B.C.E. is to be seen in the British Museum. The scene was much copied later by classicizing painters. *(Le Louvre, Paris)*

S hakespeare is something of a biographical enigma, but everyone knows that he is the favorite son of Stratford in Warwickshire, England. There is no other candidate or claimant for his place of birth—unlike for the authorship of some or all of his ("his"?) plays. Several ancient Greek cities, by contrast, lay claim to being the birthplace of Homer, Greece's equivalent of the Bard, and the dispute has never been resolved. The large island city of Chios has a claim better than most.

By the late fifth century the pioneer historian Thucydides could dare to explicitly measure his prose account of a great war against that of his epic forerunner, and challenge his statistics. Yet there is still an immense reserve of awe and respect in Thucydides' allusive quotation of a passage from an early Greek hymn to Apollo of Delos which contains the well-known reference to "the blind man from Chios." That blind man was widely assumed to be Homer himself, not least because a court poet who plays an important role in the *Odyssey* was also represented as being blind. And so the legend of the blind bard developed, of the prodigious verse

HOMER

By the time this bust was crafted, no one knew what Homer had really looked like—if indeed there had been a real Homer. But the Greeks were all familiar with the traditional hymn to Apollo of Delos, which referred to its composer as "a blind old man from Chios," and Thucydides (3.104) was not alone in attributing the hymn to Homer himself. In the *Odyssey*, the bard who had sung for Odysseus at royal command in the never-never-land of Phaeacia was likewise physically disabled but spiritually empowered—"the Muse had taken his sight from him, but in compensation she had given him the gift of entrancing song." *(Vatican Museum)* composer who lacked physical sight but was full of mental and spiritual insight, and who served as the conscience and guide of the ancient Greek people.

The *Iliad* and *Odyssey* are the first two works of European literature, and also the first two masterworks of European literature. But when we talk about the identity of the poet—or poets—who created them, history, properly speaking, does not really come into it. There is simply not enough of the right kind of evidence. The general consensus among the experts today is that there was a single monumental composer of each epic, though he was not necessarily the same person in each case. But what really matters is not so much his identity but that he, whoever he was (or they were), was a composer of verse in a very different sense from, say, Shakespeare.

Both the *Iliad* and the *Odyssey* are traditional oral epics, the ultimate outcome of a process of several centuries of oral composition and transmission of songs composed and preserved, for the most part, without the aid of writing. Somewhere along the line, towards the end of it, writing did of course have to enter the picture. Was our monumental composer himself literate? Or did he somehow dictate the monumental versions of the combined lays to a literate scribe or a small army of such scribes? Was the Greek alphabet developed when, where, and how it was precisely in order to record these monumental compositions? That last hypothesis may seem extravagant, but it has been seriously argued and indicates the unique place in the Greeks' collective social imagination that the two epics instantly came to occupy.

Saga, it has been well said, presupposes ruins. The sagas of the united Greek expedition to Troy and the ten-year siege it took to recover an adulterous Greek queen, and of the further ten years of wandering by one of the Greek chieftains before he could at last return to his kingdom and to his queen on a small and rocky Mediterranean island, probably originated in a period when the Greeks stood in dire need of consolation. The glory days of late Bronze Age Mycenaean Greece (c.1500–1100) had ended in tears, with widespread destruction of fortified sites and wide dispersal of population. Instead of palaces, the "big men" of those dark centuries between about 1100 and 900 lived in little more than glorified huts. Literacy disappeared along with luxury. In order to escape to a new life, Greeks crossed the Aegean to occupy the western seaboard of what is now Turkey, and sailed to set up new homes as far east as Cyprus. They also became more separated from each other, as long-distance trading ventures became less profitable and frequent, and in their isolation and weakness the communities turned in on themselves.

In such reduced circumstances poets could, as it were, keep the home fires burning with uplifting tales of heroic deeds by men of the past who were bigger, stronger, more adventurous, and in every way more admirable than their impoverished and demoralized descendants. So was born the epic ideal, the aristocratic and heroic striving "ever to perform outstanding deeds, and to be better even than the best," as Homer puts it. This was an ideal that outlived the time of its creation in the eleventh or tenth century B.C.E. by a long way, surviving even the rise of a relatively meritocratic and democratic ideal of existence in the fifth century B.C.E. It was somewhere roughly midway between those two periods that the monumental Homeric epics were crafted, and that "Homer" in this sense lived, in what has been called the Greek Renaissance of the eighth century B.C.E.

During this time the Aegean Greek world experienced a general economic, social, and cultural renewal, of which the Homeric epics in their monumental form are not the least.

Trade contacts were renewed and intensified with both east and west. Oriental luxury goods found their way to mainland Greece, at the same time that Greek traders struck out west and established permanent settlements as far away as the bay of Naples. A clay wine goblet made on the island of Rhodes was just one of the trade goods that ended up in a Greek grave on Ischia in the last quarter of the eighth century B.C.E. But this particular vessel has a special point of interest. It was inscribed with letters of the newly discovered Greek alphabet, which was based on borrowings from a Phoenician model. The forms of the letters used were those developed on the island of Euboea, from where the settlers of Ischia had come. And the letters were used on this vessel to write Greek verse, including a line in hexameter meter, the meter of the Homeric epics. What is more, the lines of verse make a clear allusion to a famous article described in the *Iliad*: the drinking cup of old man Nestor, a huge precious-metal goblet. The owner of the far humbler clay vessel that accompanied him to his grave on Ischia had a nice sense of humor: Nestor's cup was all fine and well, he said, but it lacked his own cup's aphrodisiac properties—whoever drank from his would be instantly seized by uncontrollable desire for Aphrodite, that is, sexual intercourse! So we see that by the last quarter of the eighth century B.C.E. not only were the Homeric epics widely current, but they were current in an entirely new world.

But whereas the Greeks who had emigrated eastwards in the eleventh and tenth centuries went in small family groups as isolated individuals, those who set off for south Italy and Sicily from the middle of the eighth century onwards went as members of organized political ventures, official foundations. The self-governing *polis* had been born. The *Iliad* and *Odyssey* are set in distant, far off times and a conscious effort was made by the poets to retain some degree of authenticity. For example, the leading characters are represented as kings who live in palaces and fight with bronze weapons, as did the Mycenaean rulers of the Late Bronze Age. But during the period of oral transmission of the epics, kings lost their palaces and indeed their positions as kings, and bronze weapons were replaced by iron ones. Archaeologists refer to this period of Greek history (or protohistory) as the Early Iron Age. These changes could not be introduced centrally into the poems without wrecking the epics' plots, but nevertheless they do creep in at the edges, so to speak, especially in the many poetic similes, the function of which were precisely to make the past comprehensibly vivid by likening it to familiar contemporary experiences.

It is thought that Homer (whether one or two) was a poet with a special talent for this sort of contemporary updating, for the interweaving of old and new. But above all he had a prodigious talent for creating a monumental narrative, for imposing on a heterogeneous and shapeless mass of traditional materials the discipline of narrative unity, rigorous selection, and a determined focus on a single main plotline: in the *Iliad* the anger of Achilles, in the *Odyssey* the nostalgia—literally the pains experienced in a voyage of return—of the King of Ithaca. The siege of Troy traditionally lasted ten years. The *Iliad* ignores all apart from a few weeks in the tenth year and doesn't even tell the story of Troy's fall! As well, many heroes besides Odysseus experienced painful *nostoi* after the capture of Troy, and Odysseus as king of rather remote and under-resourced Ithaca was not in the big league of prime-time heroes. Yet by concentrating on Achilles and Odysseus Homer was able to create immortal, imperishable tales.

In summary, the *Iliad* (over 15,600 lines) tells of the working out of the anger of Achilles within the context of a massive Greek expedition against the Asiatic city of Troy. Achilles

AJAX WITH BODY OF ACHILLES

Greek myths were not only sung or recited but also depicted in a variety of visual media, from the 8th century B.C.E. onwards. Here, on an Athenian vase of about 570 B.C.E. that was exported to Etruria and buried with its owner, the many mythological scenes include this powerful vignette of Ajax (in Greek *Aias*) carrying the body of the mighty warrior Achilles *(Achilleus)*. Despite his great feats of slaughter, alas, or perhaps because of them, Ajax went mad, killing animals as if they were human enemies and finally falling on his own sword. Sophocles's tragic play on the theme survives to this day. *(Museo Archeologico, Florence)* personally had little or no stake in the motivation or outcome of the expedition, but he had the highest possible stake in the preservation or magnification of his status as the greatest Greek hero-warrior. So when Agamemnon of Mycenae, overall commander of the expedition, deprived him of booty including a lovely young woman that he considered rightfully his, he went into a heroic sulk, refusing to fight until Agamemnon made suitable restitution and amends. The immediate result was that the Greeks began to look as though they would fail to take Troy and be driven back home in disgrace. Not even the intervention of Achilles' best buddy Patroclus, who put on Achilles' armor and led out Achilles' own troops, could make any significant difference, except in the sense that it was the death of Patroclus and the stripping of his armor from his corpse that made Achilles decide to fight again. But not for the Greek cause, which he identified anyhow as the personal cause of Agamemnon and his brother Menelaus, whose wife Helen was the ostensible origin and object of the whole Trojan saga.

Instead, Achilles fought for himself and his frustrated sense of self-worth. In so doing he scaled the heights and plumbed the depths of the heroic condition, killing Hector in single combat before the walls of Hector's own city but then dragging not only Hector's corpse but his own humanity in the mire, as he tied the corpse to his chariot, dragged it around and around the city walls, and then refused it due burial rites. Only at the end of the *Iliad*—and this is Homer's masterstroke—is Achilles allowed to rediscover the humanity buried beneath the truly epic self-regard. The climactic scene in which Hector's aged father Priam entreats Achilles for the return of his eldest son's corpse and nerves himself even to place his hands within the hands that had killed his son—that is the purest and highest literary art.

The *Odyssey* (some twelve thousand lines) never quite achieves such sublimity or profundity, yet it is no less great for speaking more to the everyday concerns of the common—or at any rate, less socially elevated—Greek man (and woman). As in the *Iliad*, the social situation that provides one of the *Odyssey*'s chief plotlines is the violation of the sacred (being under the protection of Zeus) duties of hospitality. While Odysseus is away, 108 suitors infest his home, eating and drinking at his expense, for twenty years. Odysseus' wife Penelope and son Telemachus, who grows to manhood during his father's absence, are forced to sit more or less idly by and watch the gruesome spectacle.

Penelope, of course, is not without resourcefulness; indeed, her feminine version of cunning intelligence is almost a match for that of her legendarily resourceful husband, Odysseus "of the many wiles." Her variation on the traditional feminine function of weaving—she unweaves during the night what she has woven during the day of her aged father-in-law's funeral shroud—is intended to arouse the listener's and later reader's admiration. The way in which, at the end, after the eventual reunion, she tests whether Odysseus really is who he says he is is an almost Sherlock Holmes-like piece of detective investigation. Yet the epic remains the saga of Odysseus rather than Penelope, and his wanderings are fundamentally, like the anger of Achilles in a very different way, an exploration of Greekness, of how a Greek man should behave.

Achilles tests and establishes the Greek ideal through excess. He was too angry, too self-regarding, too narcissistic, insufficiently public-spirited or communally minded. Not for nothing does the Shield of Achilles, commissioned by his immortal mother Thetis from the Olympian smith Hephaestus, depict two cities, one at war, one at peace. The famous passage describing this shield (more recent imitators include W.H.

Auden) is from the second half of the eighth century B.C.E., and probably one of the latest in the work. From then on, the city or *polis* was to be the framework of Greek thinking about political and other social and individual values. As for Odysseus, his encounters with gods, goddesses, other immortals, barbarians, cannibals, and sundry monsters before his finally decisive encounter with Penelope's grossly immoral suitors are designed to show up the proper limits of social, religious, and cultural behavior in the hugely and disconcertingly expanded and potentially terrifying Greek world of around 700 B.C.E.

Homer, the man, is unrecoverable, though he may well have looked and behaved something like Demodocus, the blind court poet of Alcinous, king of the utopian land of Phaeacia, who brought tears to Odysseus' eyes as he sang so sweetly and movingly of the fall of Troy. Homer is sometimes called the Bible of the Greeks. Insofar as the Hebrew Bible was a national epic for the Jews, the comparison is appropriate. But the significance of Homer for the ancient Greeks, as for us, is rather that of a cultural icon. In his epics, all human—and inhuman and superhuman—life was to be found: if you wanted to know how to be a politician, a general, a family man, a lover, there was some passage or scene or book of Homer that could teach you, if you only knew where and how to look.

CHAPTER 2

SAPPHO
OF LESBOS

PORTRAIT OF A
YOUNG GIRL OR SAPPHO
Pompeiian Freso

Sappho does not refer to her own appearance in her poems, and later biographers were forced back on speculative invention, making her out as short and dark (in other words, just like very many ancient Greek women). Our fresco-painter has represented a strikingly handsome woman in a suitably intellectual pose, stylus poised as she contemplates her next lines. *(Museo Archeologico Nazionale, Naples)*

Plato, the puritan, wanted to exclude even Homer, along with all other imaginative literature, from the standard educational curriculum of his ideal city, because Homer told immoral tales out of school. The vast majority of Greeks, fortunately for us, did not share this opinion. But that does not mean that he was insensible to poetry's charms. Indeed, Plato wrote poetry himself, and good poetry, too, to judge from what little survives. One of Plato's more persuasive literary judgments, if correctly reported, was his view that there were not nine Muses but ten, the tenth being Sappho. The Muses in Greek mythology were the patrons of the arts; Hesiod, a contemporary of the monumental composition of the Homeric epics, claimed to have had a personal encounter with them in their favored terrestrial dwelling on Mt. Helicon in Boeotia. One of the nine, Erato or "Loveliness," was the patron of the sort of lyric poetry that Sappho composed. For Plato in effect to equate Sappho with Erato was the highest compliment he could possibly have paid her.

Sappho is one of those extraordinary human figures who lend their names to some cultural practice, as of course did

Plato to "platonic" love. "Sapphic" as an adjective is a description of a particular (and complicated) verse meter; some of Thomas Hardy's earliest poetry, for instance, was written in sapphics. As a noun, now obsolete but once full of cultural charge, a sapphic was what we would today call a lesbian or gay woman, one whose sexual proclivities are more or less exclusively homoerotic. The term "lesbian" also comes from Sappho, whose home was originally Eresos and later Mytilene, two of the five Greek cities on the large island of Lesbos, where she was born sometime in the second half of the seventh century B.C.E. But Sappho's lesbianism—if indeed one can call it that—was, like all Greek homosexuality, of a different kind, existing in a different social and political context.

As in the case of Homer, so for Sappho historically reliable biographical details are virtually nonexistent, though it may come as a surprise to some to learn that in her extant poems she mentions by name a daughter (and so presumably had a husband) as well as a brother, besides a number of apparently very young girls. These she calls *parthenoi*, the technical term for Greek girls who were not yet deflowered through marital intercourse, and the presumption is that they were at the upper age-limit of *parthenoi*, that is, immediately pre-nuptial. Sappho both refers to the marriages of these girls and is known to have written wedding-hymns, possibly as a gift to her former associates.

But what exactly was the nature of her relationship with them? In an even more homophobic age than our own, the late Victorian era when the term "homosexuality" was invented (it is first reliably attested in English in 1890), those who wanted to rescue the reputation of Sappho the brilliant poetess from the taint of Sappho the sordid sapphic liked to think of her as a kind of headmistress of a finishing school for respectable young ladies. We need not now feel obliged to sublimate or suppress the frank homoeroticism that is to be found, for example, in her hymn to Aphrodite, the goddess of sexual love, which is the only poem of hers that survives complete. But how, then, are we to reconcile that with her having had a daughter? One useful way is to look at her poems sociologically, to view them in the wider context of Greek homoeroticism, male as well as female, in the later seventh century, and in particular within the context of her undoubtedly aristocratic background, while making allowance for the specifically Lesbian (in the geographical and political senses) society in which she lived.

In Homer there is no explicit homosexual or homoerotic behavior. Later Greeks such as Aeschylus certainly read Homer's account of the relationship between Patroclus (the elder man) and Achilles in terms of the standard pederastic institutions of their own day, but strictly that was reading into Homer's text what is not actually there. So either Homer was being deliberately reticent, for whatever reason, or pederasty on the fifth-century model known to Aeschylus had not yet been devised at the time of the *Iliad*'s monumental composition. It is hard to say which interpretation is correct. So far as the contemporary evidence goes, visual as well as verbal, however, what we now tend to think of as the standard form of "Greek love" between an adult male and an adolescent or younger adult male was probably a new cultural invention of the seventh century B.C.E. Certainly, it fit in well with the new development during that century of phalanx fighting between massed ranks of heavily-armed infantrymen (hoplites), success in which depended to a high degree on intimate male bonding and the creation of a peculiarly masculine and martial esprit de corps.

The Spartans were the masters of this new, hoplite craft, and it is no accident that at Sparta the pederastic system of male bonding was most highly developed; indeed, it was systematically imposed across the board through the state-run

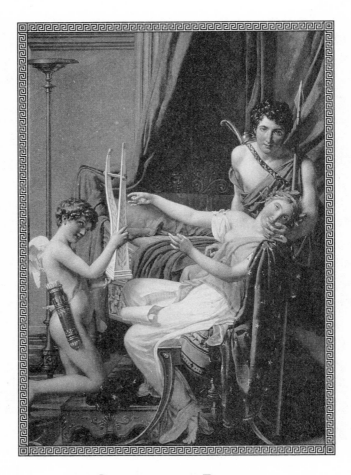

SAPPHO AND PHAON

Jacques-Louis David

Sappho's poetry lived on, an authentic testament, but
around Sappho the woman there grew up all sorts of
myth and legend. One of the less enchanting, to a
modern feminist reader, anyway, told of how Sappho
fell madly in love with Phaon the ferryman, a true
hero who had once ferried none other than a disguised Aphrodite for nothing. Her love unrequited,
however, Sappho threw herself to her death from
some high rocks. *(Hermitage Museum, St. Petersburg)*

educational curriculum that minutely controlled the life of a Spartan boy between the ages of seven and eighteen. Moreover, although Sparta was a sex-segregated society, like all other Greek cities, the state supervision of children's upbringing was extended also to the girls, who were apparently put through some kind of chiefly physical educational program parallel to that of the boys.

Sparta was, however, unique in all Greece in having such a state-imposed educational system and in extending state control of upbringing to girls as well as boys. Conclusions reached on the basis of a study of Spartan institutions cannot therefore easily be transferred to other Greek cities. Yet there is a special reason for wanting to do so in the case of seventh-century Lesbos, the Lesbos of Sappho. For the same-sex emotional bonding within a broadly educative framework of ritual passage from girlhood to marriage and motherhood that we see in Sappho's poems offers something of a parallel in the private sphere to the Spartans' public cycle, and it is striking that on Lesbos female beauty was given the same sort of public attention (via beauty contests) that was characteristic of Sparta, traditionally the home of the most beautiful Greek women. (Helen of Troy, after all, was a Spartan.)

At any rate, some sort of ritual or rite-of-passage framework seems to make the best sense of Sappho's relations with the girls she praises ecstatically and frankly lusts after. There were no homosexuals, in our sense, in ancient Greece, precisely because homosexual gratification and heterosexual gratification were not seen as diametrically opposed but as complementary and, normally, sequential. The adolescent male who functioned as the junior partner in a pederastic relationship with a senior adult male, and who went on to play the role of senior partner himself, would then normally proceed to marriage and a sexual life of predominantly or exclu-

sively heterosexual gratification, not least in order to reproduce. So, we may presume, did Sappho. What is a little odd,
though, even in comparative Greek perspective, is the existence on Sappho's Lesbos of quite such a strong female parallel to the male homoerotic/pederastic ritualized life-cycle of
Sparta and elsewhere. Still, if that was what helped crucially
to stimulate and liberate Sappho's poetic genius, we can only
be grateful for it.

Besides the hymn to Aphrodite already mentioned, two other
poems, or rather fragments of poems, stand out, and I quote
them in full (in Josephine Balmer's sensitive translations):

> It seems to me that man is equal to the gods,
> that is, whoever sits opposite you [female]
> and, drawing nearer, savors, as you speak,
> the sweetness of your voice
>
> and the thrill of your laugh, which have so stirred the heart
> in my own breast, that whenever I catch
> sight of you, even if for a moment,
> then my voice deserts me
>
> and my tongue is struck silent, a delicate fire
> suddenly races underneath my skin,
> my eyes see nothing, my ears whistle like
> the whirling of a top
>
> and sweat pours down me and a trembling creeps over
> my whole body, I am greener than grass,
> at such times, I seem to be no more than
> a step away from death;
>
> but all can be endured since even a pauper...

There are no known portraits of Sappho in marble, but this sculpture of a Muse seated with her tortoiseshell lyre *(kithara)* leaning against her might very well be taken for a representation of Sappho, the "tenth Muse," as Plato charmingly called her. *(James Pradier, Musee d'Orsay, France)*

"Burning Sappho," indeed, as Byron brilliantly called her: such intensely personal feeling, so intensely if economically rendered, though not always in terms that our culture can easily understand. Why exactly should she be "greener than grass," or "paler than grass," as an alternative translation would have it? To understand that completely would require deep familiarity with the Greeks' cultural encoding of color and color terms.

More immediately accessible, perhaps, is this:

> Some an army of horsemen, some an army on foot
> and some say a fleet of ships is the loveliest sight
> on this dark earth; but I say it is what-
> ever you desire:
>
> and it is possible to make this perfectly clear
> to all: for the woman who far surpassed all
> others in her beauty, Helen, left her husband -
> the best of men -
>
> behind and sailed far away to Troy; she did not spare
> a single thought for her child nor for her dear parents
> but [the goddess of love] led her astray
> [to desire . . .]
>
> [. . . which]
> reminds me now of Anactoria
> although far away,
>
> whose long-desired footstep, whose radiant, sparkling face
> I would rather see before me than the chariots
> of Lydia or the armor of men
> who fight wars on foot . . .

A contemporary male poet, Alcman of Sparta, dared to rank the value and pleasure of music and song against those of the battlefield, but only a female poet, surely, could have thrown the entire male baggage of war out of the window and not merely set against it but ranked above it that which (whatever or whomever it might be—the Greek relative pronoun is in the neuter case) one desires. And where many male Greeks, from the poems of Homer on, bitterly blamed Helen for her dereliction of wifely duty and gross breach of hospitality etiquette, Sappho not only exonerates her but actually justifies her decision to follow the promptings of her heart—or loins. This is subversive countercultural stuff. And then, instead of proclaiming her own Helen-like love or lust for some man, it is for the girl Anactoria (a truly regal name in Greek) that she personally longs, and, in case the hearer or reader had forgotten, rubs salt in the wound by restating the love-war comparison.

What we do not find in Sappho, as we do in her contemporary and countryman Alcaeus and other lyric and elegiac poets of the Archaic era such as Solon of Athens (see pp. 67–70), is much about politics. That is hardly surprising, since it was strictly men's business. But one suspects that Sappho's implied rejection of the priority of the political would have been considered strong meat indeed in antiquity, or even poison, depending on the point of view. Today, she somehow seems to speak to us with renewed urgency, intimacy, and congeniality, but we must not forget that we are obliged to view her life from a distance and through a pretty thick cultural screen.

CHAPTER 3

CLEISTHENES
OF ATHENS

This fine Athenian red-figured drinking cup *(kylix)* of c. 470 B.C.E. was designed to be used in the symposium (see Diotima's chapter). The scene depicted here is not absolutely certain, but it looks as though it could represent the counting of votes at an ostracism. A minimum of 6000 votes had to be cast altogether, and the "candidate" whose name was written on the largest number of potsherds *(ostraka)* was the unlucky winner of this reverse election and obliged to go into exile for ten years. *(Ashmolean Museum, Oxford)*

On the ancestry of the Athenian leader Cleisthenes hangs a tale, told at length and with brilliance by Herodotus as part of his account of the distinguished aristocratic Athenian family to which Cleisthenes belonged. Once upon a time (actually around about 575 B.C.E.), there was a king (actually a tyrant) named Cleisthenes of Sicyon, a city in the northeast Peloponnese. He had a daughter, Agariste, whom he wished to marry off. So he, as it were, advertised the post of son-in-law, and twelve suitably aristocratic Greek suitors put in an application. For twelve whole months the twelve candidates were submitted to intense scrutiny by their prospective father-in-law, to see whether they measured up to his exceptionally demanding but conventionally aristocratic standards.

Above all, Cleisthenes was interested in the candidates' athletic prowess and in their social skills, especially how they performed under pressure in the characteristic upper-class social institution of the symposium. Literally, a symposium meant a drinking-together, but there would normally be food consumed in common before the serious drinking began, and often there would be sex during and after the drinking, either homosexual sex with one's drinking mates and especially with one's own particular erotic partner, or with hired prostitutes known as flute-girls since they were supposed to sing for the symposiasts' supper as well as provide more coarsely sexual services. Admission to such exclusive drinking groups in early Greece was jealously guarded, the rules of each club were carefully observed, and membership in the smartest available set was eagerly sought.

After almost the whole year of testing had elapsed, and the time for decision was approaching, two candidates for the hand of Agariste had emerged as top of the list, both Athenian: Megacles son of Alcmeon (it was a mark of aristocratic status to include one's patronymic in one's full name) and Hippoclides son of Tisias. And so it came down to the wire, with Cleisthenes staging an almighty binge. Megacles performed with his usual unruffled impeccability. Hippoclides, though, passed beyond the tipsy stage to outright shameless drunkenness. In vino veritas: his true rather vulgar nature, and a good deal else, emerged as he indulged in increasingly libidinous dance steps (including what Herodotus enigmatically calls "Spartan figures"). Finally, in the ultimate scandal, he stood on his head on a table and waggled his legs violently in the air. Since Greek men did not wear much in the way of modesty-defending underwear, his shamelessness was there for all to see. Cleisthenes was not just surprised but insulted and outraged by Hippoclides' presumption. "Hippoclides," he thundered, "you have danced away your marriage." To which Hippoclides allegedly replied: "it's all the same to Hippoclides." Megacles (a name meaning "great in fame") duly collected his prize and some time after sired our Cleisthenes, named, as was customary, after a grandfather.

The Athenian Cleisthenes would have heard some version of the above tale as he grew up and had no doubt drawn the appropriate conclusions about socially correct behavior. Equally instructive to him would have been his father's later dalliance with a Greek tyrant, this time an Athenian called Pisistratus.

ATHENS AROUND ABOUT 600 B.C.E. had been in the throes of a severe economic, social, and political crisis. A mediating arbitrator was urgently required, and opportunely Solon, aristocratic and rich but also a man of exceptional vision and moderation, had emerged. He produced for Athens its first comprehensive set of political rules and regulations, over-hauling the constitution, reining in the grasping plutocrats, and giving a decent measure of power and responsibility to the moderately well-off non-aristocrats. He even provided some legal protection from exploitation to the humblest of Athenian citizens. (With hindsight, some of these measures can be seen as crucial to the eventual success of Cleisthenes' democratic reforms a century later, though that was hardly what was in Solon's mind.)

By trying to please almost all, Solon ended up displeasing many, and he felt obliged to leave Athens for a cooling-off period. His rules and regulations, though, remained in place and for the most part were observed for a good number of years, until, indeed, shortly after Cleisthenes' birth in about 570. During the 560s a combination of external and internal pressures led to a showdown faction-fight between three leading Athenian nobles and their supporters, whose power bases were located in different parts of Athens' unusually large city-territory of Attica. One of the three, Pisistratus, an aristocrat who claimed descent from Homeric royalty, at first emerged as the victor, seizing sole power as tyrant in defi-ance of Solon's constitution through a combination of low trickery and political and military prowess. But he failed to

SOLON

Solon of Athens, who flourished in the decades on either side of 600 B.C.E., is much more than just a name. For the ancients, he ranked as one of the Seven Wise Men, thanks to his practical political wisdom. But he fires our imagination too, since he enshrined his ideals and programs in elegant elegiac verses. Like Hesiod, he appealed to the Muses for inspiration, which came to him not least in the political poems in which he justified his reforms and warned of the consequences—"foul slavery," "internal strife," "public ruin"—if they were not strictly observed. *(Uffizi, Florence)* establish a solid enough foundation for a lasting tyranny and was soon forced into temporary exile.

A few years later, perhaps around 555, he tried again with a new strategy: if you can't beat them, join them. He first concluded a marriage-alliance with one of his two main rivals, Megacles, by wedding his daughter, Cleisthenes' sister. Megacles then helped Pisistratus to resume his tyranny, thus making Cleisthenes both the grandson and the brother-in-law of a tyrant. But the alliance soon deteriorated, partly because Pisistratus allegedly refused to practice conventional sexual intercourse with his wife (presumably because he didn't want to run the risk of having more sons—he already had three), and the loss of Megacles' support meant a second loss of tyrannical power.

The third time, Pisistratus really took his preparation for a resumption of power seriously. For ten years he built up his resources, tapping old or establishing new connections abroad, largely with a view to gaining the financial resources with which to pay the mercenary troops he needed to re-establish and maintain himself as ruler of Athens. In 546 he judged that the time was ripe. He landed in east Attica, not far from Marathon, where he had family connections and estates, and won a decisive battle over the forces of loyalist resistance. To provide himself with something like a screen of legitimacy for what was in fact a naked seizure of power by military force, he put about the story that none other than Athena herself (in fact, an unusually tall young Athenian woman dressed in armor and riding in a chariot) was personally escorting him back home, as if the Athenians of 545 were living at the time of the *Odyssey*. Such was the enduring authority of Homer. Pisistratus was now able to establish himself firmly as tyrant for the rest of his life, some eighteen years, and to hand over the "succession," as it were, to his eldest son Hippias.

This is where our Cleisthenes enters the picture. Under Hippias's overall tyranny, as under his father's, the old constitutional forms laid down by Solon had continued to be formally observed. All that was required was a certain amount of "fixing" to make sure that the "right" people occupied the relevant political posts, above all that of Archon (the nine ruling posts appointed annually to carry out the most important administrative and, especially, judicial tasks). Thanks to a documentary inscription excavated in the Athenian Agora by the American School of Classical Studies in the 1930s, we know that in 525 the man appointed to be chief Archon was our Cleisthenes, now the head of his Alcmeonid family. At some point the Alcmeonids and the Pisistratids had patched up the quarrel of the 550s, or at least Cleisthenes had decided that it would be politic for him to appear to acquiesce for the time being in Hippias's still quite young rule.

A dozen or so years later, the honeymoon for Hippias was over. A convoluted aristocratic plot involving a homosexual couple (Aristogiton and Harmodius) resulted in the murder of Hippias's younger brother, Hipparchus, who had been associated with him publicly in the tyranny. Hippias understandably treated this as a plot against himself and, according to the handed-down tradition about him, he turned into the stereotypical vicious tyrant, killing or exiling opponents, treating the defenseless citizenry harshly, and, not least, showing an unpatriotic willingness to ingratiate himself with Greeks who were vassals of the increasingly threatening Persian empire to the east (see Artemisia's chapter). (It is from behavior like this that the Greek word "tyranny" came to acquire the exclusively negative connotations of our word "tyranny.")

Among the casualties of Hippias's brutality was Cleisthenes. He may indeed have been sent into exile or gone into exile even before the murder of Hipparchus. But certainly he became the leader of the opposition-in-exile, doing all that he could to bring about the downfall of Hippias and, more particularly, one suspects in the light of his personal experiences, the end for good of tyranny at Athens. Two major and complementary means to this end recommended themselves: gaining the support of the Delphic oracle and gaining the support of the Spartans.

Apollo's chief oracular outlet at Delphi started to achieve universal Greek fame and attention in the late eighth century. Like other oracles in other cultures, what Apollo uttered through the inspired mouthpiece of his priestess did not necessarily alter the course of history. As often as not it confirmed an individual inquirer or consulting city in his or their already decided course of action. Besides, in a case of extreme doubt, it was always possible to interpret a Delphic oracle in precisely the opposite sense to its obvious meaning, which is how the legend of Delphic ambiguity (and so our adjective "Delphic") came into being. Actually, most oracular responses were perfectly straightforward, and one of the functions the oracle came to perform for a city was to set the seal of divine approval on some legislative enactment or diplomatic maneuver. The laws of Sparta, for example, were said to have been enacted under Delphic Apollo's oracular guidance, and numerous new city foundations overseas conventionally came with Apollo's divine seal of approval. It was a rather more risky procedure to try to get Apollo to intervene in a city's affairs in such a way as to overthrow the established political order. Yet this is what Cleisthenes did.

He first softened up the board that managed the sanctuary of Apollo at Delphi by offering to pay for an upgrade of the stone that was to be used in the ongoing rebuilding of Apollo's main temple from limestone to marble. He then allegedly bribed the priestess—or perhaps the priests who were responsible for,

among other things, translating the priestess's utterances into
ordinary Greek and keeping a record of them—to tell the Spartans, whenever they consulted the oracle (as they frequently
did), to free Athens from the tyranny of Hippias. This put the
Spartans into something of a double bind. On the one hand,
they had no quarrel with Hippias as such; indeed, there was
some kind of friendly understanding between them. On the
other hand, they were deeply pious and implicitly respected
what they took to be the word of Apollo (the patron, as we
have seen, of their own political system). So Cleisthenes' strategy paid off, and the Spartans did decide to overthrow Hippias,
and at the second attempt, in 510, they succeeded.

Cleisthenes, however, could not simply return from exile
and resume whatever he might consider to be the appropriate political position for himself and his deserving supporters.
He had to contend now with not only an Athenian rival but an
Athenian rival backed by the might of Sparta. A situation
something like that of the 560s recurred: a huge faction-fight
between Cleisthenes and his supporters and the Sparta-
backed aristocrat Isagoras and his. Isagoras, playing by the
traditional rules, seemed to be coming out on top at first. He
was elected as chief Archon for 508. Then Cleisthenes played
his trump card. He appealed to the *demos* of Athens; that is,
to the non-aristocratic mass of ordinary Athenian citizens,
and particularly, we suspect, to the better-off ones among
them (rather as Solon had done, but now there were more of
them, both absolutely and relatively, and they were more politically experienced and correspondingly demanding). Indeed, he did more than just appeal to them. He offered them
a new package of reforms, the effect of which was to give
them the *kratos* or decisive say in the government of Athens.
Demos plus *kratos* = *demokratia,* although that word was not
actually used for several decades after Cleisthenes' reforms of

VOTING

The effect of legal reforms championed by Cleisthenes was a redrawn political geography. Citizenship at Athens was from now on to be based on the village or ward in which one registered at the age of majority. The 140 or so villages were further grouped into three groups of "thirdings," one each for the City, Inland, and Coast area of Attica. Ten artificial "tribes," each contributing fifty councillors to Cleisthenes' new council of 500, were then created by combining one thirding from each area. The system thus put in place represented a clever combination of heterogeneity (the tribe) and homogeneity (the village).

508, democracy, or proto-democracy, was what they in effect ushered in, the world's first.

Some modern scholars, following the lead of Cleisthenes' opponents, no doubt, have interpreted Cleisthenes' reform bill as a purely factional maneuver, a way of first defeating Isagoras and then ensuring that even in the new proto- (or, for them, pseudo-) democratic order he and his Alcmeonid family would retain special power and prerogative. The contrary interpretation, however, makes sense of the fact that the new regime not only was implemented but was implemented with great success and remarkable speed. (Had it not been, it would simply have been blown away by a deadly combination of internal and external enemies.) According to this interpretation, Cleisthenes' complex and sophisticated reform package was the outcome of long and hard political thinking that took due account of Athens' political experience over the past century, and in particular of its experience of tyranny. Since that had affected Cleisthenes personally more adversely than almost any other Athenian, I do not find it difficult to see why Cleisthenes would have wished to associate himself with this essentially anti-tyrannical package of reforms, whether or not he had himself been mainly responsible for drafting them.

The key to the reform was a redrawn political geography. Citizenship at Athens, that is, entitlement to the privileges of Athenian citizenship (available to adult males only, of course), was from now on to be based on the village or ward (another sense of *demos*) in which one was registered at the age of majority. Legitimate birth from an Athenian father was also required, but not necessarily also from an Athenian mother. That would have excluded Cleisthenes, after all. There were about 140 of these villages or *demes* in all, and they were further grouped, for purposes of national self-government, into thirty "thirdings," ten to each of the three broad sectors—City, Inland,

and Coast—into which Attica was divided. Ten artificial "tribes" were thus created by combining one City, one Inland, and one Coast thirding. Each such tribe would then provide fifty councilors to Cleisthenes' new Council of Five Hundred, which would become, in effect, the administrative body of the Athenian state and the steering committee of the Assembly to which all Athenian citizens were entitled to go to vote on matters of national concern such as peace and war. The system thus put in place represented a clever combination of heterogeneity (the tribe) and homogeneity (the *deme*). It was very soon to be put to the sternest test of all: national defense.

In 506 the Spartans, unhappy both with this democratic turn and more particularly with the popular rejection of their Athenian friends (first Hippias, then Isagoras), gathered a massive expedition of their allies both inside and outside the Peloponnese. It was no doubt fortunate for the Athenians that the Spartan leadership was divided at the very top by an irreconcilable disagreement between Sparta's two kings, Cleomenes I and Demaratus. The Peloponnesian branch of the projected Spartan invasion of Athens broke up in disarray, leaving Athens free to deal with its hostile neighbors in Boeotia and Euboea, as she did with total success. But it was not only with other Greeks that Athens had difficult relations at this time.

Hippias, as we have seen, had established Persian links before, which likely contributed to his overthrow. Faced with the massive threat from the Spartans, the Athenians were not above contemplating applying to the same source for help, especially, perhaps, financial aid. When they found they did not need Persian support, they were quick to repudiate any hint that they had once been willing to treat with the Oriental superpower, and in 499 B.C.E. they made a special point of lending concrete aid to their fellow-Greeks of Ionia in their attempted revolt against their Persian suzerain. But in the meanwhile, their potential troubles from Sparta were not quite at an end. Smarting from their humiliation of 506, the Spartans called a congress of their allies and put forward a singular proposal: to restore Hippias as tyrant of Athens in the Spartan interest. Embarrassing as this was, since it contradicted their rhetoric of anti-tyrant liberationism (the Spartans were proud of never having experienced a tyrant themselves), it was a less bad option than having a confident, democratic Athens on the loose in central Greece, where it might set an unfortunate example of encouragement for the political aspirations of the *demos* in all those other cities where political power remained traditionally in the hands of the elite few, the *oligoi* (hence "oligarchy").

What became of Cleisthenes amid all this hubbub and furor during the last years of what we call the sixth century B.C.E.? We do not know, though the simplest explanation for his apparent disappearance from the political scene is that he died soon after. He would have been in his mid-sixties by then, and he had led a particularly vigorous and rigorous life. But his legacy lived on and was remembered, if not always with a warm glow of appreciation. Herodotus visited or lived in Athens around fifty years later, and among his Athenian aristocratic informants were Alcmeonid descendants of Cleisthenes as well as descendants of his opponents. Being aristocrats, none of them (apart from Pericles) was too keen on Cleisthenes' opportunist maneuver (as they saw it) of turning to the *demos*, of bringing the *demos* in from the political cold and giving it a place of honor by the fire. But they could not disguise from Herodotus the fact that, as he reported, it was Cleisthenes who "created the tribes and the democracy for the Athenians."

CHAPTER 4

ARTEMISIA
OF HALICARNASSUS

Sometimes scholars like not only to refer an object to its general class of vasepainting (Athenian red-figure ware) but also to give the painter a name. This scene has therefore been attributed to the hand of the Triptolemus Painter, who executed it in c. 480, just at the very moment of the Persian invasion led by King Xerxes. The scene would remind the Greek user of this drinking cup of his countrymen's great deeds in the Persian Wars, such as the decisive victory won by the hoplites (heavy infantrymen, like that on the Right here) over their Persian opponents at the battle of Plataea in 479. *(Trustees of National Museums of Scotland)*

The city of Halicarnassus today is called Bodrum, an international holiday center on the western, Aegean seaboard of Turkey, noted particularly for its water sports facilities. In antiquity it enjoyed a more serious image. It was especially famous for housing one of the Seven Wonders of the ancient world, the Mausoleum. This was a huge funerary monument commissioned about 350 B.C.E. for the eponymous Mausolus by his widow—and full sister—Artemisia. She was clearly a formidable lady, but though deeply Hellenized she was not actually Greek. Her Greek namesake was equally if not more formidable. This Artemisia is known to us chiefly through the *Histories* of her younger contemporary and fellow Halicarnassian, Herodotus. Like other powerful political women Artemisia was obliged at first to play second fiddle to a man, her husband. But once he was dead, she picked up the reins not only of government but of power.

The Greek word for courage or bravery, especially as displayed in battle, meant literally "manliness" (as did the Latin word from which our term "virtue" is derived). It was therefore, strictly speaking, impossible for a Greek woman to be

CYRUS THE GREAT

Of all the founders of empires Cyrus must
rank among the very greatest. The Achaemenid
Persian empire he created within the space of
thirty years outlasted him by a further two
hundred. Truly, as he and his successors styled
themselves, he was "king of kings, in many
lands"—at its greatest the Persian Empire
stretched from central Asia to the first
cataract of the Nile. *(Le Louvre, Paris)*

brave in the required military sense—or, if not impossible, at least paradoxical. But Herodotus, uniquely and with a certain amount of national pride, does not shrink from ascribing this quality to Artemisia. This was a bold move in many ways. For Artemisia displayed her true-grit Greek bravery not on behalf of the loyalist Greeks fighting to preserve their culture and independence in the Persian Wars of 480–479 but on behalf of the Persian invader. Artemisia, queen of Halicarnassus, was also a vassal of Xerxes, Great King of Persia, King of Kings in many lands. As such, she was obligated to follow him in battle wherever he might choose to order her, and in 480 the target was Greece and the goal its conquest and incorporation within the Persian empire.

THE PERSIAN EMPIRE OF THE ACHAEMENID ruling dynasty had been founded some three generations earlier by Cyrus II, also known as Cyrus the Great. (In Persian his name comes out as something like Kurash; Cyrus is the Latin form of the Greeks' approximation of his name—the Greek language lacked, as it still lacks, the "sh" sound.) Cyrus makes an honorific appearance in the national literature of the Jews because it was he who in 539 ended their exile, plucking them from beside the rivers of Babylon (see Psalm 137) and restoring them to their Levantine homeland. The Jews were not alone, though, by any means, in giving Cyrus good press. Herodotus too has few bad words for him, and the general impression his narrative conveys is that he was a wise and generous as well as a prudent and powerful ruler. Xenophon, a contemporary of the Mausoleum, wrote an entire book about him, a sort of early romance or novel in which Cyrus was represented as embodying the cardinal virtues of leadership for Xenophon's Greek readership.

Cyrus began the process of founding his empire in the 550s B.C.E. and died in 529. His son Cambyses added Egypt, so that within a generation an empire had been created that stretched from beyond the Hindu Kush in the east tó the first cataract of the Nile in the west, and embraced most of the Asiatic landmass in between, a total of some three million square kilometers. This made it the fastest-growing empire the Orient has ever seen, and one of the largest and most complex, too. It included peoples of many tongues, religions, and cultures, a plethora of terrains and geographies. To conquer it was achievement enough; to maintain it intact for some two centuries was little less than marvelous. But it all almost unraveled in the generation after the death of the founder's son.

Herodotus is the best available narrative source for what was going on in the Persian empire in the troubled 520s. But he could be no better than his sources, and he could not read what the official and unofficial Persian texts said, or indeed texts written in any language other than Greek. He had heard orally that Cambyses died in suspicious circumstances, perhaps even by suicide, possibly because he was more than a little mad. There had then reportedly been an interregnum, and a brief usurpation by a Mede, not a Persian. The Medes and the Persians, who occupied respectively northern and southern Iran, were related but distinct peoples. (The Greeks regularly confused the two, but we should not, since that would be something like confusing the Welsh and the Irish today.) This interregnum had encouraged widespread revolts from Persia by the recently subjected peoples, especially in Babylonia and Egypt. Order had finally been restored by the third Achaemenid ruler, Darius, a distant relative of Cambyses who had the key advantage of being married to Cambyses' sister Atossa (another formidable woman, who is given an important role not only by Herodotus but also by the Athenian tragic playwright Aeschylus, in his work *Persians* of 472).

DARIUS I

Cyrus's greatest successor, almost a second founder of the Persian empire, was Darius I (reigned 522–486). Cyrus's capital had been at Pasargadae; Darius built not one but two new capitals, at Persepolis (in Greek; "Parsa" in Persian), the chief ceremonial centre, and Susa, the principal adminstrative seat. Here, on this relief from the Treasury at Persepolis, Darius is shown enthroned in splendor. Before him a subject bows in the traditional greeting of respect (*proskunesis* or obeisance), indicating the unbridgeable social distance between him and his god-anointed suzerain. *(SEF)*

However, all or much of this could be just propaganda, spread in self-justification by the successful newcomer Darius, who was not in direct line of succession to the throne and found himself faced with numerous hostile Achaemenid males, the inevitable product of the royal Persian harem system. Darius, at any rate, was no mean propagandist. At Behistun in Media he had carved in the living rock a huge trilingual inscription in which he gave his version of the events leading to, or rather, as he put it, necessitating, his assumption of the throne. It was this inscription that eventually, in the nineteenth century, enabled the decipherment of the official Persian royal script and language, which scholars call Old Persian. Darius was very careful, though, to give the supreme credit not to himself but to the tutelary divinity of the Persian royal house, Ahura-Mazda, god of light. Indeed, he had himself represented in the Behistun relief seated on his throne under Ahura-Mazda's divine protection.

Whatever the truth of the official Darius version, there is no doubting that Darius was the second founder of the Persian empire after Cyrus. After suppressing the widespread revolts and establishing himself firmly in power, he carried out an administrative overhaul of the entire empire. This was divided into provinces, known in the Greek transliteration as satrapies, each under the direct rule of a royal Persian satrap or viceroy. There were at least twenty of these, and the main purpose of the overhaul was to establish just how much tribute, and what form of tribute, each was to pay annually to the two main regnal centers located in the Persian heartland: Persepolis, the ceremonial capital, and Susa, the chief administrative capital. Herodotus somehow got hold of a version of this administrative reorganization and tells us in great detail what he believed (as he was told) each of the twenty satrapies was obliged to pay during the reign of Darius (c. 522–486 B.C.E.).

He had a special reason for his interest, as we have seen: his own city of Halicarnassus was enrolled in one of them, as indeed were all the Greeks who lived along the Aegean seaboard of Asia from the Hellespont (Dardanelles) in the North to the land opposite the island of Rhodes in the south, together with those Greeks who lived on Cyprus. Interestingly enough, these Greeks had not chosen to revolt during the time of troubles following Cambyses' somewhat mysterious death. On the other hand, they did rise in revolt some twenty years later, when most of Persia's subjects did not. Herodotus's account of this revolt, the so-called Ionian revolt of 499–494, forms the prelude to his main story, the invasion of Greece led by Darius's son Xerxes in 480. The connection between those two events, the Ionian revolt and the Persian invasion of Greece, is in Herodotus a direct one. Xerxes had vowed to carry out his late father's unfulfilled intention to exact revenge on the mainland Greeks, and in particular on Athens, for first sending help to the revolting Ionians and then defeating the original Persian expeditionary force at the battle of Marathon in 490 B.C.E.

This was where our Artemisia came in. Her name is theophoric: she was named, that is to say, after a god, or rather goddess, Artemis, sister of Apollo. Artemis's birthplace and chief spiritual home was the Cycladic island of Delos; her most famous shrine was at Ephesos in Ionia, where the rebuilt fourth-century temple was another of the ancient world's Seven Wonders. Of Artemis's several functions, the most intimate for a Greek girl was that she presided over the sensitive transition from wild girlhood to tamed marriage via the achievement of puberty at the age of fourteen or so. On achieving menarche, a Greek girl would symbolically dedicate to Artemis some of her most prized girlhood possessions—a favorite toy perhaps, or a favorite article of clothing. This was to symbolize that she was leaving behind her childhood for good, and embarking on the predestined course of marriage and motherhood.

The father who named her Artemisia and who arranged her marriage was called Lygdamis, a name he shared with the contemporary tyrant ruler of the Cycladic island-city of Naxos. But Artemisia's mother came not from Halicarnassus but from Crete, a telltale sign that she was from an aristocratic background, since Greek aristocrats were in the habit of contracting marriage-alliances with powerful men in other Greek cities and sometimes even with non-Greeks. By 500, which was roughly when Artemisia was married, it was unusual for a Greek city to be ruled by a hereditary king. Sparta was the most outstanding oddity in this respect—doubly odd, in fact, because it actually had two hereditary kings. (See Cynisca's chapter.) But Halicarnassus was a slightly odd Greek city in that it contained a mixed population of Greeks and non-Greek Carians, who seem to have intermarried, or at any rate sometimes had close relationships with each other. Perhaps in this slightly old-fashioned outpost of Hellenism the tradition of monarchy inherited from the Homeric epics had been artificially preserved longer than was normal elsewhere in the Greek world. At any rate, Artemisia's husband (whose name we don't know) seems to have been a legitimate king, rather than a usurping tyrant such as Lygdamis of Naxos and a number of other Greek tyrants whom Persia supported and perhaps even sometimes imposed on their subject Greek cities.

Artemisia's husband, however, died young, too soon for their son to succeed him, so Artemisia did so herself. She was not the first Greek widow of a king to step literally into her deceased royal mate's shoes, nor was she the last. But she did so with a particular élan and éclat. When Herodotus introduces us to her, he does so in a description of Xerxes' review of his combined forces as they mustered in the northern Aegean early in 480. The Persians' invasion had been long prepared, and longer meditated. The invading force was, so the Greeks liked to believe, preternaturally huge—1,700,000 land troops, and 1207 ships. These figures tend to be scaled down today to something of the order of 80 to 100,000 and 600 respectively. Consciously imitating his ultimate literary model, Homer, Herodotus gives us both a roster of Xerxes' land forces and a Catalogue of the Ships and their commanding officers on the Persian side, including among the admirals a full brother and half-brothers of Xerxes, the admiral-in-chief, himself. In over-all command of the subject Greek and Carian ships was one of the half-brothers, another son of Darius. Herodotus next mentions by name ten captains, including three Carians. Then, at last, as the climax of his Persian fleet review, the spotlight falls not on a man, but on a woman: "I pass over the other captains, but I do find occasion for admiration in Artemisia: she, though a woman, served in the expedition against the Greeks."

Artemisia led the men not only of her native Halicarnassus but also of the offshore islands Cos and Nisyros and of Carian Calydna (or perhaps Greek Calymnos). Halicarnassus itself had provided five ships, presumably triremes of the latest design: that is, three-banked oared warships powered by some 170 rowers, carrying a crew and marine force of twenty to thirty more, a complement of some 200 in all. These five Halicarnassian ships, Herodotus proudly records, were second in repute only to those provided by the crack Phoenician seamen of Sidon. It was in fact the Phoenicians of modern Lebanon and Cyprus who provided the core of the Persian imperial east Mediterranean navy, and who were expected to win for Xerxes the naval part of his amphibious campaign against the Greeks. But their captain Artemisia, in the best Homeric heroic tradition, was not just a doer of deeds. She was also a speaker of words, with a head on her shoulders, a head that

XERXES

As often, the son and successor Xerxes
(486–465) proved a far lesser man than his
great father Darius. Apart from his disastrous
attempt to extend his empire across the
Aegean to engulf mainland Greece, Xerxes's
reign was also afflicted by serious domestic
upheavals. It was therefore all the more necessary for him to insist on the maximum of royal
pomp and circumstance, as in this relief showing him larger than life under the welcome
shade of a parasol. *(Giraudon/Art Resource)*

uttered wise counsel: so wise, indeed, that, if we are to believe Herodotus, Xerxes valued her advice above that of all his
other captains.

After the great review described above, Xerxes himself advanced south with the fleet to a position off the coast of Attica,
the territory of his major enemy and principal target, Athens.
But on the way a great storm blew up and wrecked a good
many of his ships, thereby evening up the odds a bit in any future encounter with the loyalist Greek, mainly Athenian, navy.
This was providential, as Xerxes' land army under Mardonius
had scythed its way through the Greek resistance, such as it
was. Greek tradition made a very great deal of the heroic self-
sacrifice of the Spartan King Leonidas and his three hundred
Spartans at the pass of Thermopylae, but that could never
have been intended as more than a holding operation and
temporary morale-booster, a sort of placatory sacrifice to ensure divine support for the main Greek resistance which would
have to take place at sea.

In due course it did: at Salamis, a small island off Attica. In
command of the Greek fleet was Themistocles, a man of immense cunning and resourcefulness as well as strategic far-
sightedness. It had been he who had dissuaded the Athenians
from granting themselves each a cash-bonus when the state-
owned silver mines of Laurium yielded a lucky strike in 483,
and persuaded them to put the money instead into the building of a spanking new fleet of two hundred trireme warships.
This was democracy, specifically Cleisthenic Athenian democracy, government by mass meeting, in successful operation.

Themistocles had his enemies, many of them, both at home
and abroad, and they were powerful figures. Against them he
mobilized the power of the ordinary people of Athens, who
voted to ostracize Themistocles' opponents one by one. (In an
ostracism a voter entered a potsherd, *ostrakon* in Greek, with

the name of the politician he wanted to see exiled from Athens
for ten years written, painted, or scratched on it. The "candidate" with the most potsherds cast against him was the "winner" of this devastatingly successful reverse election.) In
recognition of his foresight, his acumen, and his cunning
Themistocles had been placed in overall command of the
naval arm of the Greek resistance. It took all his powers to
keep the force together before any fighting actually took place.

However, Themistocles recognized that even with this new
fleet of warships at his disposal, the only hope of a Greek victory was to fight the larger and superior navy of the Persians in
narrow waters, where the effectiveness of their practiced sea-
manship and lighter ship construction would be minimized.
According to the prevailing Greek account, Themistocles re-
sorted successfully to trickery in order to lure Xerxes into the
narrow strait between Salamis island and the Attic mainland.
But actually he may not have had to work quite as hard to persuade Xerxes as the patriotic Greek sources imagined. Xerxes
as much as Themistocles needed a thumping victory. He was
anxious to achieve that sooner rather than later. Narrow waters or not, he would probably have imagined that the result of
any head-on clash with the puny Greek naval forces would be
a foregone conclusion. Unfortunately for Xerxes, the battle of
Salamis went all Themistocles' way.

Like a great painter with an eye for detail, Herodotus places
highlights on the broad canvas of his stirring battle description. One of these artfully picked out Artemisia. She found herself in a tight spot. The Persian navy had fallen into utter
confusion. Looking for a way out of the straits she was in (in
more than one sense) she found her exit blocked by friendly
ships, including one from Carian Calynda. With an Athenian
trireme hot on her tail she displayed that quality of cunning intelligence so admired by the Greeks and calmly rammed the

GREEK FLEET AT SALAMIS

This imaginative re-creation of the great sea-battle off the coast of Attica in 480 nicely captures the furious clash of oared warships in a confined space, even if the details are less than entirely authentic (triremes had three banks of oars, for example). "At once a ship struck its bronze ram against one of ours. At first the floodtide of the Persian army resisted, but the Greek ships encircled them, and the sea was no longer to be seen, brimming with corpses"—so the messenger brought the bad news of Persian defeat to Xerxes in Aeschylus's tragedy *Persians* *(Mary Evans Picture Library)*.

Calyndian ship as if it were one of the enemy and sank it with all hands. The captain of the pursuing Athenian trireme was certain that the sunken ship was an enemy ship and quite naturally inferred that Artemisia's ship was not what it had seemed: either it was in fact a loyalist Greek ship or it was a Persian ship which had decided to change sides. Either way, it was no longer to be considered a target, and Artemisia was allowed to make her getaway.

To cap it all, this scene was personally witnessed by Xerxes, seated atop his specially erected golden throne overlooking the straits. Recognizing Artemisia's ship by its standard he also inferred that the ship she had sunk had been an enemy ship, and reportedly uttered the immortal comment: "My men have become women, and my women men." A remark with which Herodotus, in this one particular case of Artemisia, entirely concurred.

Queens are, of course, not as other women are. Artemisia was almost as much of a rarity among Greek womanhood as was Hatshepshut, the sole Egyptian woman pharaoh. Artemisia's combination of coolness under fire and sage advice off the battlefield represented a male ideal at odds with the more passive, even submissive model of womanly virtue that Greek men liked to have offered up to them for their contemplation and delectation in imaginative literature and the visual arts. But she is by no means the only feisty Greek woman we are going to meet in these pages.

CHAPTER 5

PERICLES
OF ATHENS

PHEDIAS AND THE FRIEZE
OF THE PARTHENON
Lawrence Alma-Tadema

Greatest, or at any rate most lasting, of Pericles's many achievements was the construction of the Parthenon on the Athenian Acropolis between 447 and 432 B.C.E. In this lushly imaginative reconstruction the Dutch-born Sir Lawrence Alma-Tadema (1836–1912, the painting is of 1869) pictures Pericles, accompanied by Aspasia, being shown a close-up view of the Parthenon's inner frieze by its likely overall designer, Phidias. We, like Alma-Tadema, rate Phidias a great artist, but many Greeks would have considered him a mere tradesman—no one, Plutarch reported, would actually want to *be* Phidias, however much they admired his work. *(Birmingham Museum and Art Galleries)*

Pericles, son of Xanthippus and Agariste (who bore the same name as her grandmother, the mother of Cleisthenes), was an Athenian aristocrat, born around 493 B.C.E. This was an important conjuncture in the history of his city. The Persians were coming. Indeed, by aiding their fellow-Greeks of Ionia (on the western Asia Minor seaboard) to revolt against the Persian empire in 499, the Athenians had virtually invited them in. "Remember the Athenians" is what Persian King Darius supposedly asked to be reminded daily. In 490 it was he who launched the expedition that was to meet defeat so famously at Marathon, in a battle that John Stuart Mill—almost as famously—declared to be an event more important in English history than even the Battle of Hastings!

For men of Pericles' station and class it was normal to contract deep and lasting relationships of hospitality and mutual aid with aristocrats in other Greek cities, occasionally even with non-Greeks. Out of such permanent and hereditary relationships might naturally come an exchange of one of the men's most prized possessions: their women, who were given in marriage, or rather, were given for the purpose of forging a

PERICLES

True portrait sculpture, as opposed to idealiz-
ing heroic images, did not begin in Greece until
well after Pericles's death (in 429). But this famous image of Pericles, a copy of an original
usually attributed to Cresilas, was apparently
true to life in one respect—Pericles was said
to have been embarrassed by the onion shape
of his cranium and to have insisted on having
himself depicted wearing a helmet.

politically and socially profitable marriage-alliance. It was therefore not uncommon for aristocratic Athenian men like Pericles to have a foreign mother or other female blood-relations, normally from another Greek city, as we have seen in the case of Pericles' relative by marriage, Cleisthenes. Pericles himself, however, was responsible for putting a stop to that practice at Athens for good, by the law on citizenship which he proposed to the Athenian Assembly in 451 B.C.E. This law made it illegal for the son of an Athenian father and non-Athenian mother to become an Athenian citizen. What prompted Pericles to propose that popular measure is still disputed. What matters here are the implications of Pericles' law for his own personal life.

When in his twenties, Pericles seems to have done the conventional thing for one of his station and class—married an Athenian girl of similar background and upbringing to his own. That her name is unknown to us is not as surprising as it may at first seem. It was a universal male Greek protocol not to broadcast the identity of one's wife or other female relatives. Indeed, it was considered bad form even to talk about them outside the immediate family circles. Gossip like that could attract unwelcome attention or attentions, especially sexual, from unrelated and possibly hostile males.

Nor is it entirely remarkable that Pericles, after fathering two sons upon her, should have divorced this nameless wife. Divorce in fifth-century Greece carried none of the theological or moral stigma that it does in a Christian or post-Christian society, and in practical terms it was relatively simple to arrange. The key condition was that the husband should pay back what remained out of the dowry paid, usually in cash, by the bride's father or guardian. Then he was legally free to divorce his wife unilaterally and remarry. One reason for doing this might be that she had failed to produce a child, or at any rate a male child. Another was that she had committed adultery, in which case the husband was legally required to divorce her. What is remarkable in Pericles' case is not only that his wife had produced two male children and not (so far as we know) committed adultery but also that Pericles should have chosen not to remarry.

Pericles was lord and master (*kyrios*—the word later used to mean "Lord" in Byzantine Christian liturgy) of a substantial estate (*oikos*, whence our "economy"). Typically, one of the key functions of a rich Athenian's wife was to be the faithful guardian of "the things inside," as the current phrase went; that is, to manage the household stores and personnel on a day-to-day basis, ensure that husband and children were properly fed and clothed, oversee the children's upbringing with the aid of a slave tutor (*paidagogos*, our "pedagogue"), take responsibility for the accommodation, health, and labor of this and other household slaves, and so on.

Pericles, one might have thought, would have been manifestly in need of a wife. Instead, he chose to leave all his household management chores to a male slave (or perhaps freedman). This was an arrangement he seems to have positively if unconventionally favored, for he continued with it even after he had acquired, if not a lawfully wedded Athenian wife, something at least as pleasing to him: Aspasia.

If Pericles' private life was, or became, unconventional, that was entirely in keeping with the tenor of his public life. His first known appearance on the public stage was almost literally that: at the age of twenty or so he acted as financial sponsor for the group of tragedies by the great Aeschylus that included the still surviving *Persians*. Unusually, Aeschylus had chosen for its theme not some mythical affair from the dim and distant past but an event as contemporary and an issue as alive as could possibly be imagined: the defeat of the Persians by the Greeks, and especially the Athenians, at Salamis in 480, just under eight years before.

It is not possible to infer for certain Pericles' political outlook at this early stage, nor, indeed, is it certain what line, if any, Aeschylus himself was taking. But the burning Athenian political issue of the day was Themistocles, the author of that great naval victory, and Aeschylus came as near as the conventions of tragedy would allow to actually naming him. Moreover, the play treats the victory in an entirely positive way (however much tragic pity for the defeated Persians Aeschylus may also have wanted to evoke in the audience). Since Pericles was later to follow very much in the tracks of Themistocles so far as his naval policy and attitude to the development of the Athenian empire were concerned, it's not entirely fanciful to read Pericles' sponsorship of the *Persians* as a youthful political statement of intent.

Not that the play and Aeschylus' victory in the tragedy competition availed Themistocles much: he was soon ostracized and, hounded by both the Athenians and the Spartans, sought and received honored refuge in the Persian empire, where he died a pensioner of the Great King himself, Artaxerxes I, the son of his great enemy Xerxes. Treachery? Enlightened self-interest? The Athenians treated it as the former and would not allow him to be buried back home. Any canny politician would therefore have been quick to disassociate himself from any taint of connection with Themistocles. In fact, so blackened did Themistocles' name become that Thucydides, ever the revisionist, felt it necessary to rehabilitate his legacy, quite correctly, from a purely objective historical point of view. It was indeed, as Herodotus had said, the Athenians who, after the gods, were most responsible for the Greeks' repulse of the Persians in 480–479, and of the Greeks, as even the Spartans grudgingly conceded, none was owed

PERICLES

more individual credit than Themistocles. Once, a man from the tiny Aegean island of Seriphos (a member of Athens' post-war naval alliance and empire) is supposed to have bearded Themistocles and said to him: "You're only famous because you come from Athens." To which the great man replied, devastatingly: "But no one would have heard of you, my friend, even if you had been an Athenian!"

Pericles' role in possibly wishing to exploit the *Persians* politically is of course just speculation. What is not is that a decade later Pericles made his entry on to the political stage as the junior adjutant of a radical democratic reformer, Ephialtes. The package of reforms that the two men championed and got passed by the Assembly amounted to the completion and consolidation of the democratic reforms introduced by Cleisthenes fifty years before. The last vestiges of the pre-democratic aristocratic order were swept away, and the Athenian People were allowed, or rather required, to rule of, by, and for themselves, above all through the Assembly and the popular jury-courts.

The one measure with which Pericles himself is specifically associated is the introduction of payment for service as a juror; not a large fee, by any means, but enough to provide equivalent financial compensation (or more) for a day spent away from the fields or marketplace or workshop by an average, that is to say poor, Athenian citizen. In the version of his famous Funeral Speech written up by Thucydides, Pericles tells the Athenians that it is not poverty which they should consider shameful but the refusal of even a poor man to make his public political contribution to the running of the state. Every year the Athenians empaneled by lot a permanent pool of six thousand Athenians from which were selected, again by lot, the juries who sat on 150 to 200 days a year to judge every conceivable public or private lawsuit, often ones with directly political content and effect. To enable that to happen, with the large shift in political experience and power that it entailed, was perhaps the single major contribution made by Pericles to the development of democracy at Athens.

Indeed, this imaginative use of public funds is the chief characteristic of Pericles' political career, apart from his persuasive oratory. Certainly, he was not the greatest general or admiral, and his supposed famous last words—"no Athenian ever put on mourning because of me"—must have rung a trifle hollow even then. Rather, he is remembered for his effective pursuit of a coherent and consistent line of public policy—especially foreign policy—over some two decades: anti-Persian within limits, remorselessly anti-Spartan, limitlessly pro-Athenian in the broadest, imperial sense. And his most lasting legacy is his invention and supervision of Athens' extraordinary building program, reflected most tangibly in the long shadow cast by its crown jewel, the Parthenon.

One contemporary source wrote that persuasion sat on Pericles' lips. Persuasive public speech was nothing new in Greek culture. Homer's heroes had had to excel "in counsel as well as in war." What was new was that the decisions rhetoric persuaded people to make were now made by the masses rather than the elite, by thousands of ordinary Athenian citizens, as many of them as were able or willing to make the trek to the Pnyx hill (where the Assembly met once a month, or more frequently in case of emergency). Despite the technical developments occurring in the theory and art of rhetoric in Pericles' own day, no amount of book learning could compensate for a weak or inexpressive voice, a lack of authoritative presence, slowness on the feet in verbal repartee, and a failure to command the issues.

Typically, the sorts of issues facing the Assembly were matters of religion, public safety or defense, and the food supply.

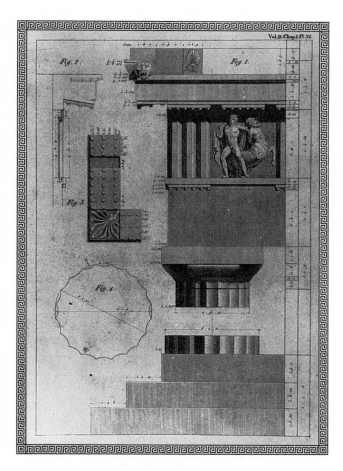

THE PARTHENON

Stuart and Revett

Greek temple architecture, as represented by
the Parthenon above all, exerted a powerful influence on neoclassical building design from the
early 19th century on. This drawing is designed
to help the student recognize the main archi-
tectural members—column, capital, entabla-
ture, triglyph, metope—of the Parthenon's
Doric order.

These were the three issues that took priority on any agenda drawn up for the Assembly by its steering committee, the Council of Five Hundred (chosen annually by lot). Religion speaks for itself: the Greek city was a city of gods as well as men, and claiming to know the gods' will or be in a position to secure their favor was an important part of a statesman's public profile and persona. Security issues bulked large, as Greek states were so often at war, with other Greek states more often than with non-Greek foes like the Persians. Athens, for example, was at war with someone, on average, two years in every three throughout the fifth and fourth centuries, and at peace for no more than a decade at a stretch. The food-supply was also a major problem since by the mid-fifth century the population of Attica (Athens' home territory) had already outstripped its capacity to feed them all—perhaps a quarter of a million people, including slaves (eighty to one hundred thousand, mostly non-Greek), resident aliens (mostly Greek), and the citizen population.

From time to time, however, the occasion arose for making decisions on matters other than the narrowly pragmatic or utilitarian. One such occasion, the chance not just of a lifetime but of an epoch, came in about 450, and Pericles was brilliantly positioned to exploit it. His popularity and authority were high. He had just passed his citizenship law. His chief political rival, Cimon, had recently died. Athens, now at the head of a great maritime empire (thanks importantly to Cimon), was in a position to make a favorable peace, or at least an empowering détente, with Persia, with whom she had been at war continuously for the past thirty or so years. The "peace dividend" was there in the public coffers to be spent: by Greek standards a truly huge surplus that had been built up from the external tribute of her allies and from a variety of internal sources such as taxes and fines. The question was, on what should it be spent, if indeed it should be spent at all (rather than hoarded against a rainy day—the return of the Persians in force, for example).

It took all Pericles' persuasive powers to make the Assembly agree that a huge chunk of this available surplus should be spent over a number of years on rebuilding the religious structures of the Acropolis and elsewhere, many of them destroyed by the Persians thirty years before and left unrestored as a kind of warning and inspiration. It then took—and this is less often noted—all his financial acumen and sheer bureaucratic dutifulness to oversee the entire program, ensuring that the sums came out right, the money allocated was appropriate for its designated purposes, and that it was properly spent—neither wasted nor filched. Pericles himself acquired a reputation for total financial probity, and especially for his imperviousness to bribes (the Greek word for that was the same as their word for "gifts"—one man's gift was another's bribe, depending on the point of view). This was utterly crucial to the success of the venture, although associates of his, including the chief sculptor Phidias, did not escape charges of peculation.

The Parthenon, whatever else it was and is, is hence a gigantic monument and memorial to Pericles' achievement as a statesman. So too was the Odeion (our Odeon) or Singing Hall, an imaginative building of unique design set up against the slope of the Acropolis. This was where plays were previewed before the annual Great Dionysia festival and where trials were occasionally held. And so were a number of other great buildings both in Athens (e.g. the Portico of Zeus the Liberator) and outside (the temple of Poseidon at Sunium, for instance, where Byron, among many others, carved his name). Thucydides brilliantly predicted that a future traveler to Athens, on seeing the ruins of these extraordinary monuments, would tend to overestimate Athens' true power.

Thucydides' comment was prescient in more ways than one, for controversy raged then, as it still does today, over Pericles' attitude towards Sparta and in particular over his role in leading Athens into the great and ultimately disastrous Peloponnesian War (431–404). Some political opponents and other hostile critics held that Pericles had various personal reasons for wanting Athens to be at war with Sparta. Perhaps the least persuasive version of this view claimed that in war a politician is better able to disguise his crimes against the people. Other critics held, and some hold today, that Pericles was a warmonger, pursuing excessively aggressive policies that were bound sooner or later to so antagonize Sparta as to leave her no viable option but to declare war on Athens.

Defenders of Pericles, of whom Thucydides would not willingly yield first place to anyone, take the opposite view. Not only was Pericles personally so morally upright that he could not possibly have had any purely personal reasons for wishing to involve Athens in war, but, they aver, he had so accurately estimated the dynamics of Sparta's foreign policy that he had prepared Athens adequately and in time to meet the predicted Spartan onslaught and had prescribed the correct strategy to follow, a mainly defensive one with important offensive elements. In this view his only mistake, if it could be called that, was to underestimate the enormous cost of a lengthy war of attrition such as the Peloponnesian War turned out to be. (Just four years after his death the Athenians were apparently obliged to treble the tribute of their allies in order to take account of that.)

Yet no statesman can absolutely control or fine-tune a tense and fraught international diplomatic situation. War conceivably could have been avoided; at any rate, it was not as inevitable as his supporters, including Thucydides, have suggested. But, above all, Pericles was not as all-powerful as he has too often been represented, as he was, for example, many centuries later by Plutarch.

Within two years of the start of the Peloponnesian War it all seemed to be going horribly wrong for the Athenians. Their lands had been devastated by two Spartan invasions. The Great Plague (typhus, perhaps, we still can't be sure) had struck them, which apart from causing death also sowed wide-spread demoralization, not least because many ordinary Athenians were conventionally pious and interpreted the disease as divine nemesis for some previous religious offense. So demoralized were they in fact that in 430, contrary to Pericles' express wishes, they decided to send a deputation to Sparta to see what peace terms the Spartans might be willing to offer. Naturally enough, the Spartans interpreted this as a sign that their own war strategy was working and declined to negotiate, which only demoralized the Athenians further, so much so that they did what would have been unthinkable only a few months earlier and deposed Pericles from his office as General and served him with a presumably quite hefty fine. So much for the view that Pericles was the uncrowned king of Athens—here was direct democracy in action, literally with a vengeance.

Happily, the gloom quite soon lifted, the Spartans' war strategy began to look as hollow as Pericles had said it would, the effects of the plague slackened, and the Athenians, when the next elections came around, re-elected Pericles. Unhappily, though, the plague was to have the last word on Pericles' fate. He had not died directly from it, not as quickly as had his two sons, but he did die in the autumn of 429, in his early to mid-sixties, from its debilitating aftereffects.

His loss to Athens was in Thucydides' view so great that he considered it to be the cause above all other causes of the city's eventual defeat in the Peloponnesian War twenty-five years later. Thucydides, himself a member of the old aristocratic elite and by no means an unqualified supporter of rad-ical direct democracy, found himself in a quandary. How could he square his huge personal admiration for Pericles with the undoubted fact that Pericles was a convinced demo-crat who had increased the power of the People over the elite? His solution was to blame it all on Pericles' successors as (mis)leaders of the People. Whereas Pericles had led the People and not been afraid to tell them what they should do in their own interests and so the interests of Athens, the suc-cessor "demagogues" had merely pandered to the masses, at the expense of their betters, in order to gain and maintain personal influence and authority. Plato, however, took a dif-ferent view, though he was born after Pericles' death and was in no position to form an authoritative opinion. To him Peri-cles was simply a class traitor who, as his mouthpiece "Socrates" colorfully put it, bribed and fattened up the popu-lace like a pastrycook dispensing sweet goodies. Posterity has sided with Thucydides.

CHAPTER 6

ASPASIA

OF MILETUS AND ATHENS

ACHILLES SLAYING PENTHESILEA, THE AMAZON QUEEN

On this Athenian black-figure vase the greatest of Greek heroes is shown killing the queen of a tribe of women, or near-women, who seem to have filled the ordinary Greek man with terror. Amazons were oriental barbarians (non-Greeks), who did without the company of men for most of the time (getting together with them for procreative purposes only as and when *they* saw fit) and exchanged normal women's tasks for the masculine arts of war. Thank Zeus, they were but figments of the Greeks' mythical imagination... *(Michael Holford/British Museum)*

A ristotle in his great work of applied political theory, the *Politics*, let the cat out of the bag: women are half the human race. For some of us that might be considered a cause for celebration, or at any rate no bad thing. But for Aristotle, as for many adult Greek males of his day, it was a problem. In his quintessentially sexist view women just did not have what it takes to be citizens in the full, actively political sense. By the standards of that ideal role model, always and without exception male, women just didn't measure up.

This was not exactly women's fault. It was simply a fact of their unalterable nature (in Greek *phusis*, from where our "physical" and so on are derived). This doomed them to being forever inferior to men. Biology *was* destiny, in this chauvinist view. Of course, Greek women would on average and on the whole be reckoned by Greek men to be better than non-Greek women, and free women superior to slave women. And one's own female relatives would normally be considered at least as good as the female relatives of any other man. But, still and all, women were inferior to men, categorically so.

The richer a Greek man was, the more he could afford to keep his womenfolk out of sight of unrelated males in purpose-built women's quarters, such as those depicted on this women's toilette-box *(pyxis)*. There, aided by their female slaves, they were supposed to practice the typically feminine arts of clothes-production, which both contributed to the household's economy and (it was hoped) kept them out of trouble. *(Le Louvre, Paris)*

All sorts of reasons were brought forward to account for this ineradicable deficiency of female nature. For many Greeks, it was all put down to the gods, who had bestowed many gifts on Pandora, the mythical first woman they collectively created (the Greeks' equivalent of Eve)—but not good sense. In her insatiable curiosity Pandora opened the storage jar containing all the world's evils as well as blessings, and so let out the evils that would afflict poor mortal mankind for ever. It was a woman then, typically, who was held responsible for such things as plague, disease, and hunger.

Aristotle, the leading scientific thinker of his day (and of most days), took a different line. Women's inferiority, he held, was partly due to biology, partly to psychology. On the one hand, women were, he believed, sort of incomplete or deformed males. They lacked men's crucial, literally vital, reproductive capacities. In an era before the discovery of ovulation and the true appreciation of women's equal contribution to reproduction, this belief was not quite as extraordinary as it may seem to us. Although some ancient theorists held that women too produced "seed" of some sort, the standard ancient view was that the woman's womb served merely as a passive receptacle for the male's active semen. This was by way of an agricultural analogy with the earth, understood as female, that received from the (male) farmer the active, germinating seed.

On the other hand, women's minds were also for Aristotle crucially defective. He was prepared to accept that women could reason logically—an obvious enough fact to most of us, but not a widely shared view among ancient Greek men. Yet women still were, he thought, sadly incapable of translating their reasoning processes into equally rational actions. They were, in other words, simply too emotional and passionate by nature.

We are today all (too) familiar ourselves with similar traditional negative stereotypes. But at least most of us are aware most of the time that that is what they are—gendered constructions that conveniently serve male interests of power and authority, not disinterested scientific descriptions of the world as it is, of the true state of nature. Aristotle, though, despite his native brilliance, probably could never have been persuaded to see that what he regarded as objective scientific fact was actually just social ideology or myth. Ideology about gender was too potent a force, too deeply ingrained in the ancient Greeks' male-dominated worldview, for it to be comfortably displaced, let alone dispensed with altogether.

This does not mean that the male-centered worldview was not questioned or laughed at by Greeks. It most certainly was, searchingly by philosophers and other thinkers in the relative privacy of academic institutes such as Aristotle's own Lyceum school and humorously by playwrights such as Aristophanes in the public space of the theater. Nevertheless, this questioning and ridicule did not materially affect the everyday lives and beliefs of ordinary Greeks. Here the situation remained hierarchically lopsided, probably for two reasons above all others.

First, anatomy really was destiny for an ancient Greek woman in a far more tangible way than we would think either possible or desirable today. Coping with menstruation and its associated social, religious, and health problems was difficult enough. Coping with childbirth was literally a major life crisis and one all the more frequently faced given the absence of effective methods of contraception. Some modern demographers have even estimated that in order to merely keep an ancient Greek population stable, fertile women of reproductive age would each have had to have produced on average nine children (of whom perhaps less than half would typically reach adulthood, let alone a ripe old age). In fact, infant mortality was so prevalent that it was the custom not to name a newborn—and so give it a social identity—until nine days after birth, and perhaps no more than one infant in three would survive its first year. Maternal death in or soon after childbirth was also a depressingly common experience in the ancient Greek world. It was no wonder that Greek girls were betrothed as early as was practical and normally married off as soon after puberty as possible, because that way, the Greeks thought, they would maximize each girl's reproductive potential. In these circumstances it was easy enough, though wildly unfair, for Greek men to regard women as the congenitally weaker sex. This fixed opinion was massively reinforced by the Greeks' cultural attitude to war. To them, war was inevitable and normal, whereas peace, however desirable in theory, was in practice an interruption of the state of war. War, in the words of the brilliantly individual thinker Heraclitus of Ephesus (c. 500 B.C.E.), was "the lord of all and the father of all; some he makes free, the others slaves." In the pithy phrase of Thucydides, the war historian par excellence, war was "a violent taskmaster." But, above all, war for the Greeks was gendered, by definition men's work. This was because the quality of courage, bravery, or pugnacity that was required for fighting the sort of wars the Greeks fought was in their vocabulary "manliness" (*andreia*).

It was therefore literally impossible for a Greek woman to be "brave" in the relevant martial sense—without a certain irony or paradox, anyhow (as we saw in our discussion of Artemisia, above). Of course, women could show a sort of courage on occasion, for example when defending themselves, their family, or their property from a hostile intruder. But that was not the same, and not given the same social credit, as the courage required on the field of battle, where the crucial dimension of mental self-control came into play as well as instinctive or passionate self-defense.

Condemned thus by their bodies to suffer the pangs of menstruation, defloration, and childbirth, and irredeemably lacking because of their "nature" the quality of martial manliness, Greek women were inevitably the second sex. Of course, there were exceptional Greek women—there are always exceptions—either in terms of their sheer mental and physical endowments or in terms of their capacity to exploit the given social conditions and relations between the sexes to their advantage. In classical Greek terms that meant exceptional freedom from the norm of male domination.

It is not difficult to think of such exceptional females in Greek myth, from the goddesses Hera, Athena, and Aphrodite down to heroines of epic poetry and tragic drama like Helen of Troy and her sister Clytemnestra. It is harder to conjure them up in real Greek life. It helped, for example, if one were a queen, or the widow of a king, like Artemisia. But Aspasia was not royal by either birth or marriage, though the fame she achieved after death, as in life, is enough to make her count as royalty of a sort.

ASPASIA CAME ORIGINALLY FROM Miletus on what is now the Anatolian or west coast of modern Turkey. Her name means something like "joyful," a name chosen by her father, Axiochus (a name that also appears in Alcibiades's family), who also decided that she should be reared by her mother and his male and female household slaves. But Aspasia owes her remembrance, and notoriety, to her association with the second most important man in her life, Pericles of Athens. The very fact that she was able to contract that association, and to maintain it without compromising her individual identity, speaks worlds for her unusual intellectual and social attributes.

The fact that we know Aspasia's name, and not that of Pericles' former, lawfully wedded wife, is the first revealing thing about her. It is because she was the subject of malicious gossip, not only in the barbershops and market square behind cupped hands but even outspokenly in the full public glare of the Athenian comic stage. The biographer Plutarch (writing some six hundred years later) reported that Aspasia was actually taken to court and prosecuted for impiety by a well-known comic dramatist. But that is almost certainly a misunderstanding by a non-contemporary and non-Athenian with rather a solemn outlook on life of the nature of Athenian comedy. Such licensed slandering of the great and good was part of the comedian's normal stock-in-trade. Another comic misrepresentation of Aspasia was easier to see through. In one play of about 430, by which time her relationship with Pericles was almost twenty years old, she was portrayed as Helen of Troy to Pericles' Paris in order to heap mud on Pericles for his alleged personal responsibility for causing the outbreak of the Peloponnesian War.

The absolutely standard—and standby—dramatic representation of her is rather more interesting, not least because it has fooled and continues to fool so many commentators and historians. Aspasia was put on and put upon as being a *hetaira*. The term meant literally a female comrade (Homeric heroes had called each other "comrade" and the term was still current in fifth-century Athens, if sometimes with rather dubious political associations of right-wing politics), but by Aspasia's day it had acquired the meaning—positive or negative according to social class and sexual taste—of upscale prostitute or (to take a rough modern equivalent) courtesan.

One of the most amusing variations on this comic theme in a play that survives comes in Aristophanes' *Acharnians* of 425. Here the protagonist recalls a story he's heard about the true origins (read: unbelievable tale) of the Peloponnesian War. Once upon a time, in fact only six years ago in real life, some young blades from the neighboring city of Megara, which was an ally of Athens' chief enemy Sparta, had crossed the border into Athenian territory, entered the city of Athens itself, and stolen two hookers from the best little whorehouse in town, run by none other than . . . madam Aspasia.

Eccentric and exceptional though Aspasia undoubtedly must have been, she was not and could not ever have been a *hetaira*. Her relationship with Pericles, with whom she lived and had a child as well as acting as surrogate foster-mother to Pericles' ward Alcibiades, was the equivalent of that of wife to husband, though legally she would have been counted as his *pallake* or concubine. ("Common law wife" might be an appropriate English equivalent.) As for Pericles, he went out of his way to show that, despite his aristocratic birth, upper-class upbringing, and great wealth, he did not go in for the normal off-duty relaxations of his social peers, partying with *hetairai* (or worse) at drinking binges (dignified with the name *symposia*). He was, to that extent, a man of the People.

Why then did he not (as they used to say) make an honest woman of Aspasia by marrying her? Here irony overlays eccentricity and exceptionalism. He was debarred from marrying her precisely by the law on citizenship proposed in 451 by . . . himself. Formally, perhaps, he could have contracted a second-class marriage with a foreign, non-citizen woman, but that would have gone against the spirit of a law that was very popular with the electorate on whose favor and goodwill he depended as a leading politician in a radical democracy. If anyone could not afford to be seen to go against that law, it was its author.

Given that his law made even a permanent liaison with such a woman as Aspasia dubious—hence all the comic obloquy discussed above—why did Pericles choose to flout convention and invite such criticism by openly living and procreating with her, instead of remarrying a second Athenian wife? The second part of that question is easier to answer than the first. He

already had two legitimate sons, who were therefore automatically heirs to his name and estate unless he should choose to
disinherit them, which would have been most unusual. Part-
ible inheritance—equal division of the estate between all legitimate sons—was the rule in Athens as in most of classical
Greece, and however desirable it was in some ways for a man
to have a number of surviving adult sons, at his death that
would mean excessive subdivision of an estate with all sorts of
unpleasant economic, social, and personal consequences.

Common gossip had a ready answer to the first part of our
question: sexual passion. In what the Greeks considered an
unmanly and slavish way Pericles, it was said, was uncontrollably in love with Aspasia, who unnaturally (for a woman)
held the whip hand over her male lover. After two decades of
cohabitation that explanation begins to wear a little thin.
Clearly, it was not only Aspasia's body that Pericles found
stimulating and attractive, but also her mind. But that fact too
was open to criticism by satirical exaggeration. The woman
as "the power behind the throne" is a familiar trope. One
Athenian version of it appears in the dialogue by Plato called
the *Menexenus*. Here Plato's Socrates in all faux-naif honesty
attributes the writing of Pericles' famous Funeral Speech delivered in 430 (of which Thucydides preserves a version) to
the hand of Aspasia.

That, as I said, was satire. In real life Plato did have one or
two female pupils at his Academy of higher learning and
speculation, but it was only in his *Republic* utopia that he
could envisage some women, admittedly very few, being the
intellectual equals of the select men qualified to rule his ideal
state as philosopher-kings. However, the condition of their
getting together, sexually, was they did without the normal
accompaniments of real life relationships between the sexes,
that is, family life and private property. Aspasia and Pericles,

on the other hand, had lived together, had had a son together, and had enjoyed the benefits of Pericles' extensive
private wealth.

Plato's *Republic* belongs to the first quarter of the fourth century, the same period as Aristophanes' dystopian satire,
Women in the Assembly, in which Athenian women seize
power in the state and institute an authoritarian communalist
feminocracy. That was well after Aspasia's death. But she had
perhaps led the way and set the precedent of an independent,
clever woman—a terrifying thought for many men.

Not that Aspasia's relationship with Pericles was all smiles,
quite apart from the comic brickbats they had to endure. Pericles, as we have seen, had died of the Great Plague in 429.
Worse, he had been predeceased from the same cause by his
two legitimate sons, which had left him suddenly heirless. The
Athenian People, whose respect bordering on veneration for
their great leader had been demonstrated time and again over
the past twenty years or more, were equal to the occasion. By
special decree of the Assembly the son of Pericles and Aspasia, also called (defiantly?) Pericles, was formally legitimated
and naturalized as an Athenian citizen. With his parentage and
background he was exceptionally well placed to enter on the
public political career that was the normal ambition of such
young men. Thereby hangs a sorry tale.

One of the peaks of an Athenian political career, especially
in wartime, was to be elected one of the ten supreme Generals, an annual (renewable) office. In 406, twenty-three years
after his father's death, Pericles junior achieved this supreme
accolade. Sadly, he thereby got caught up in the fiasco in which
all eight Generals involved were illegally as well as unjustly
condemned to death for failing to rescue large numbers of ordinary Athenian sailors after a major and (barely) victorious
naval battle off the coast of Asia Minor. The same Athenian

ATTACK ON THE PIRAEUS

The Athenians' chief naval and commercial harbor, the Piraeus, had first been fortified under the guidance of Themistocles at the beginning of the 5th century. To no avail, in the end: In the spring of 404, Lysander and his victorious Spartan fleet sailed in to conclude the Peloponnesian War. One of the conditions he imposed was that the walls of the Piraeus be pulled down, which was carried out to musical accompaniment. Many, wrote the contemporary historian Xenophon, believed that this signaled the beginning of liberty for Greece—actually, it marked the beginning of the tyrannous empire of Sparta. *(Mary Evans Picture Library)*

People which had raised Pericles junior to the political and military heights thus cast him untimely to the depths of Hades. It would be hard to think of a more bitterly ironical twist of fate affecting any other real ancient Greek, truly a *peripeteia* (reversal of fortune) worthy of a tragic hero such as Oedipus.

How long Aspasia lived on after Pericles died we do not know, though we can only hope she was spared this ultimate maternal misery. What we can infer is that as a foreign widow with merely resident alien status, lacking the buttressing of kin, she was in an extremely vulnerable social position. And we do know that she chose the obvious solution of remarriage, or rather the contracting of another non-marital union with another prominent (albeit less so) Athenian politician.

The lucky man she chose for herself this time was Lysicles. He too became a target of the generally conservative comic poets, but partly for snobbish reasons, not only because he was a leading democratic figure. Quite unlike Pericles, he seems to have drawn his wealth from some sort of commercial activity to do with sheep rather than from his ancestral landed estates. Lysicles, in other words, belonged to the breed of "new politicians" that was so despised not only in the broad and perhaps not entirely serious humor of the comic stage but also in the desperately sober historical pages of Thucydides.

The backgrounds of such men as Lysicles accurately reflected the transformation of Athens over the half century since the Persian Wars into the major commercial center of the Aegean and indeed the east Mediterranean world as a whole. Aspasia, it would appear, remained the progressive woman to the last.

CHAPTER 7

SOCRATES

OF ATHENS

DEATH OF SOCRATES

Charles Alfonse Dufresnoy

During his imprisonment, Socrates engaged daily in philosophical conversations with his followers, and in the *Phaedo* Plato portrays him on the day of his death discussing the possibility of the soul's immortality and drinking the hemlock that would kill him with a complete lack of concern, an idea also conveyed by Charles Dufresnoy's portrait of the great philosopher. *(Galleria Palatina, Palazzo Pitti, Florence)*

The problem of reconstructing the life of Socrates has been compared to that of writing the life of Christ. Neither wrote a word of his teachings, which have been preserved, not always consistently, in the writings of their disciples. The parallel extends further, for some. Socrates, in one influential view, was a martyr, put to death for his beliefs. So too, less controversially, was Christ. Whether or not one finds this parallel helpful or even suggestive, Socrates is certainly the most famous philosopher of all antiquity, and altogether one of its most famous figures. Which makes it all the more frustrating for us historians that we really have so little solidly reliable evidence to go on. But what little there is is worth its weight in gold, because it comes from such fascinating sources—Aristophanes and Xenophon as well as Plato—and because Socrates' life and the way he lived it both coincided with and brilliantly reflected one of the most golden epochs of all human intellectual and cultural history.

Socrates' social origins were relatively humble. His father was a stonemason, but probably one well enough off to own a workshop and employ slave assistants. His mother was at

SOCRATES

Socrates was famously ugly, seeming to recall facially the half-human, half-animal satyrs who in Greek myth were the lewd attendants and drunken companions of the wine god Dionysus. But in a dialogue written by his less famous pupil Xenophon, Socrates is said to have joked that his bug eyes, though aesthetically unpleasing, were functionally superior to normal eyes, since they enabled him to see sideways as well as straight in front.

some time a midwife, which gave the cue for one of Socrates' favorite metaphors for his own intellectual activity, that of bringing to birth the embryonic thoughts of those with whom he conversed. As to what job Socrates himself did, well, the answer is he simply didn't have a proper job, at any rate not when he was devoting himself full-time to his self-appointed task of being Athens' gadfly, stinging the lazy Athenian people to make them more self-aware and self-critical. When he first came to notice, he was already in his late thirties (he was born in 469), fighting for his native city in north Greece in the early stages of the Peloponnesian War with Sparta that had broken out in 431.

By then he was married to Xanthippe, to whom the hagiographic pro-Socrates tradition has not been kind. Later in the Peloponnesian War it is possible that he took a second wife, or at any rate a concubine. The city was tending to turn a blind eye to such extramarital liaisons, such was its need to make good its mounting losses of citizens in battle. Unkind gossip, of course, blamed the liaison on Xanthippe's shrewishness. He next catches the public eye in 423, when he appeared by name as a leading character in a comedy by Aristophanes of which a version has survived to this day, the *Clouds*. Aristophanes' portrait of Socrates was highly unflattering and highly controversial. But it also testifies that by his mid-forties Socrates was a very well-known figure on the streets of Athens. He was indeed a thoroughly urban intellectual.

Active military service would have no longer been expected of Socrates after the age of fifty, though he seems to have remained unusually tough and fit right up to his premature death at seventy in 399. It is in a political rather than military or intellectual capacity that he next pops up center-stage, in 406 during the so-called Trial of the Generals after the battle of Arginusae. Socrates was then a member of the annual Council of Five Hundred, chosen by lot to represent his *deme* and tribe. In fact, it seems that on the very day of the trial he was, by the luck of the lottery, acting as president of the entire Council, and so presided over the Assembly meeting at which the Arginusae generals were charged with dereliction of duty. The Athenians had actually won the sea-battle against the Spartans, but it had been a Pyrrhic victory, and the generals were blamed, probably unfairly, for the unusually high citizen casualty figures.

Whether president or not, Socrates certainly refused to endorse the proposal put to the Council that the six generals present should be tried then and there by the Assembly, and tried collectively, en bloc, rather than one by one. His opposition was based on legality, and as such it was certainly correct. But there was another agenda at stake here, over and above the question of the legality of the procedure, and overriding also the question of the generals' guilt.

This trial was part of an ongoing struggle-to-the-death between convinced democrats and their equally convinced and diehard oligarchic opponents. In 411 this struggle had erupted into outright faction-fighting, and there had been a counter-revolutionary oligarchic coup led by four hundred extreme oligarchs. One of these four hundred, Theramenes, was the prime mover behind the trial of the generals in 406, presumably because he calculated that their conviction would severely weaken the democratic leadership. Paradoxically, Theramenes was able to persuade the mass of the ordinary Athenians to adopt his anti-democratic tactic, and despite Socrates they did illegally condemn the generals to death en bloc, among them Pericles, the son of Pericles with Aspasia (as we saw in the previous chapter).

Eighteen months later in spring 404, Athens was eventually forced to capitulate to Sparta's by then superior naval and fi-

1 *previous page*, "HOMER" BY REMBRANDT
Several Greek cities laid claim to being the birthplace of Homer and all of them gave
his poetry a home, since he was for all Greeks simply "The Poet." The *Iliad* and *Odyssey*
are the world's first great works of western literature, but they have often been taken
too as inimitable guides to Greek and non-Greek life. In Homer's epics, all life—human,
inhuman, superhuman—was to be found. Rembrandt was keenly aware of his classical
heritage—one of his many self-portraits shows him dressed up as Zeuxis, the famed
late fifth-/early fourth-century B.C.E. Greek painter from Southern Italy. *(Mauritshuis, The
Hague)*

2. *above*, LUIGI SABATELLI, "OLYMPUS" (CEILING FRESCO)
Greek religion was polytheistic; they believed in many gods and goddesses, as opposed
to the strict monotheism of orthodox Christianity. The Greek's loose and heterogeneous stock of creation myths went with an absence of dogma, a lack of sacred scriptures, and the nonexistence of a privileged vocational priesthood. In the mythology of
ancient Greeks, the most powerful gods and goddesses resided on Mount Olympus, as
one big but not always happy family under the watchful eye of Homer's "lord and
father" Zeus. *(Galleria Palatina, Palazzo Pitti, Florence)*

3. *previous page,* VASE DETAIL: ACHILLES VS. HECTOR
The climactic duel between Hector, eldest son of the king of Troy and heroic champion of the besieged city, and Achilles, mightiest warrior of the Greeks, is one of the poet of the *Iliad*'s most dramatic masterpieces. It has been memorably captured here in clay and paint by an artist known to scholars as the Berlin Painter, one of the greatest masters in the first generation of Athenian red-figure vasepainting. *(Michael Holford/British Museum)*

4. *above,* GAVIN HAMILTON, "PRIAM PLEADING WITH ACHILLES FOR THE BODY OF HECTOR" *(Tate Gallery, London)*

5. *right,* LEOPOLD BURTHE, "SAPPHO JOUANT DE LA LYRE"
"Burning Sappho," as Byron brilliantly called her, was the great poetess of ancient Greece. Her name leant itself to an art form (the "Sapphic" is a complicated verse meter, especially one consisting of a trochaic pentameter line with a dactyl on the third foot) and a cultural practice (as an adjective, now obsolete but once full of cultural charge, Sapphic meant lesbian) *(Musee des Beaux Arts, Carcassonne)*

6. *above*, VASE PAINTING: GREEK FIGHTING PERSIAN
Hardly surprisingly, the scene of a Greek warrior triumphing over a Persian adversary was popular in Athenian vasepainting in the years around 480: among the great deeds in the Persian Wars was the decisive victory won by the hoplites, or infantrymen, over their Persian opponents at the battle of Plataea in 479. A quiver or bowcase at the Persian's waist in this image suggests that his sword, unlike the Greek's, is a weapon of last resort. *(Trustees of National Museums of Scotland)*

7. *left*, JUSTUS VAN GENT, "SOLON"
In 508 B.C.E., Cleisthenes put into effect a set of legal reforms that marked the beginning of classical Athenian self-rule: proto-democracy. However, Cleisthenes' reforms were possible partly because of the political groundwork laid almost a century earlier by Solon, a man of exceptional vision and moderation. Around 600 B.C.E., Solon produced for Athens its first comprehensive set of political rules and regulations, overhauling the constitution, reining in the grasping plutocrats, and giving a decent measure of power and responsibility to the moderately well-off non-aristocrats. His constitutional reforms continued to be formally observed through the rule of two tyrants. *(Le Louvre, Paris)*

8. *previous page*, MEDIAN AND PERSIAN
DIGNITARIES, PERSEPOLIS, RELIEF ON
OUTSIDE OF EAST STAIR OF APANANIA
(GRAND CEREMONIAL AUDIENCE-HALL)
The Greeks seemed unable, or unwilling, to distinguish the Medes from the Persians, but though
they were both Iranian peoples and related to
each other, they had distinct histories and
retained distinct customs and practices, especially
religious. The Magi, for example, who astonished
Herodotus, were a Median, not a Persian, priestly
order. Cyrus the Great, the founder of the
Persian empire, had a Median mother, but the
empire he founded was specifically a Persian one,
ruled from Parsa (in Greek "Persepolis") in
southern Iran. Here, the Persian Great King, king
of kings, ceremonially received tribute and homage annually from the twenty or more provinces
of an empire that stretched maximally from
Pakistan to the first cataract of the Nile in Egypt.

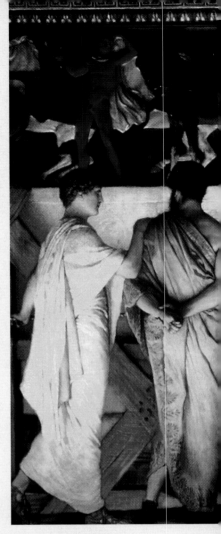

9. *left,* THE PARTHENON, as it may have looked in the time of Pericles.

10. *above,* LAWRENCE ALMA-TAMEDA, "PHIDIAS AND THE FRIEZE OF THE PARTHENON"
A vivid work by Sir Lawrence Alma-Tadema, this painting of 1869 presents Pericles, accompanied by Aspasia, being shown a close-up view of the Parthenon's inner frieze by its likely overall designer, Phidias. Alma-Tadema visited Pompeii on his honeymoon in 1863 and was captivated by the beauty of the classical remains. He spent the rest of his life recreating scenes from the ancient world in his art. *(Birmingham Museum and Art Galleries)*

11 AND 12. *above and left,* two representations of scenes from Homer's *Odyssey:* LEON BELLY'S "THE SIRENS (ULYSSES TIED TO THE MAST)" *(St. Omer, Hotel Sandelin)* and GIOVANNI STRADANO'S "PENELOPE WEAVING" *(Palazzo Vecchio, Firenze)*

13. *following page,* JEAN LEON GEROME, "YOUNG GREEKS AT A COCK FIGHT" Cock-fighting was a very popular sport in Athens, and pairs of fighting cocks frequently appear in various forms of Athenian art. The sport was apparently watched by Athenians of all ages and classes, but was perhaps particularly loved by young men, as cocks were seen as symbols of masculine aggression and sexuality. *(Musee d'Orsay, Paris)*

14. CHARLES FRANCOIS JALABERT, "OEDIPE ET ANTIGONE"

In Sophocles' *Oedipus at Colonus*—his last play, produced posthumously by his grandson—Antigone leads her blinded father (and, as they both now know to their great cost, half-brother) to sanctuary and peaceful death at Colonus, Sophocles' own home village just outside of central Athens. Sophocles' *Antigone*, which was written and staged almost four decades earlier, represents Antigone's own, far less happy end: she was walled up and starved to death by her uncle Creon. *(Musee des Beaux Arts, Marseille/Jean Bernard)*

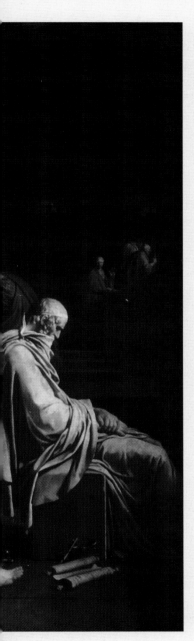

15 AND 16. "DEATH OF SOCRATES"
These two representations of the death of Socrates, by Jacques-Louis David *(left)* and Charles Alfonse Dufresnoy *(previous page)* show the death of the philosopher in heroic style. In 399 B.C.E., a small majority of Athenians in a jury of 501 were persuaded to vote against Socrates on charges of inventing new gods, not recognizing the gods the city recognized, and corrupting the city's youth. Although he was remembered more upon his death for being the teacher of traitors Alcibiades and Critias, his manner of death had a profound effect upon another of his students, Plato, who venerated him as the perfect philosopher, in constant pursuit of truth and knowledge, especially self-knowledge. *(Dufresnoy: Galleria Palatina, Palazzo Pitti, Florence; David: The Metropolitan Museum of Art, New York)*

17. *below,* RAPHAEL'S MASTERPIECE, "SCHOOL OF ATHENS," showing the philoso-phers Plato and Aristotle enagaged in disputation beneath the arching ceiling of a great basilica. *(Bridgeman Art Library/Vatican Museums and Galleries)*

18. *above,* THE CITY OF ALEXANDRIA, FLOOR MOSAIC OF SAINT JOHN'S CHURCH, GERASA, JORDAN

Alexandria was the queen of Alexander the Great's city foundings, of which there were at least six and perhaps as many as twenty. Here it is represented on a late Antique mosaic map from Madaba. What the mapmaker could not show were the great Museum and Library founded by Alexander's immediate successor as ruler of Egypt, Ptolemy I, the founder of the line of which Cleopatra (died 30 B.C.E.) was the last representative. *(Archaeological Museum, Gerasa, Jordan)*

19. *following page,* AGOSTINO MITELLI AND A. M. COLONNA, "THE TRIUMPH OF ALEXANDER THE GREAT"

The main lineaments of Alexander's extraordinary, unprecedented, and unparalleled career are agreed upon, although what drove him to such heights (and sometimes depths) must be left to speculation. Indeed, having run out of mortal men to rival, it seems as though Alexander set himself to emulate heroes (Heracles) and even gods (Dionysus). We have come ourselves to partake in this apotheosis of Alexander, as evidenced by this ceiling fresco, depicted much in the same spirit as the painting of Olympus earlier. *(Museo degli Argenti, Florence)*

nancial resources. Starvation had left Athenians dead on the streets as the result of a Spartan blockade conducted with brutal efficiency by Lysander. Athens was thereby obliged to surrender unconditionally and to assent to Sparta's terms. One current of Spartan opinion wanted to see the Athenian menace obliterated for good by wiping Athens from the map, a view endorsed by at least two influential allies, Corinth and Thebes. But the majority view, which preferred a subservient to a nonexistent Athens, prevailed, partly precisely because of Sparta's fear of those two allies, so Athens was allowed to become subject to a narrow oligarchy, or *junta*, of just thirty men aided by a board of ten to control the crucial port of Piraeus. This *junta*, backed by a Spartan garrison, behaved in such a callous way as to earn for itself the title the Thirty Tyrants. Fortunately it lasted only a year or so before even the Spartans saw that it was being counterproductive and consented to a re-establishment of democracy under close Spartan military supervision.

Socrates' attitude towards the *junta* is a fascinating study, though the evidence is rather tainted since it featured so strongly much later in his trial, execution, and subsequent recriminations. On the one hand, he did not leave Athens to join the democratic resistance or to simply avoid the *junta*. Indeed, since he stayed, it is almost certain that he was enrolled as one of only three thousand citizens granted the privileges of the new oligarchic order. (There had been at least twenty thousand citizens with full rights under the democracy in 404, and once perhaps as many as fifty thousand in the 430s and 420s.) On the other hand, when the *junta* sought to implicate him further with their policies by requesting him to arrest and inform upon a prominent resident alien, he refused point-blank. Again, legality was his sticking-point, but this time it was an oligarchic, not a democratic, legality that he was up-

holding. Many of his defenders both in his own day and sub-
sequently have not unnaturally tried to make him out to have
been at least a good Athenian citizen, and possibly also a
good democrat but they have had an uphill task: adages like
"the majority is always wrong" with which Socrates was reliably credited (or debited) are not the sentiments of a democrat, ancient or modern.

That Socrates has needed defenders is owed to two re-
motely connected attacks on him: the first, that by Aristophanes in the *Clouds*; the second, that brought officially in a
court of law by three prosecutors in 399. In the *Apology* (de-
fense-speech) written for him by Plato, Socrates is made to
refer back to the *Clouds* attack and claim, rather implausibly,
that the prejudice it aroused still clung to him twenty-four
years later.

Aristophanes was an intensely political comic playwright,
and found the perfect medium for his humor in the annual
state-sponsored drama festivals in honor of Dionysus. Consider his output during the first phase of the Peloponnesian
War. His earliest surviving whole play, the *Acharnians* of 425,
was a sort of peace-play; the *Knights* of 424 and the *Wasps* of
422, both savage attacks on the manipulation of the hood-
winked masses by their unscrupulous leaders, especially
Cleon; and the *Peace* of 421, as its name implies, quite explicitly a peace-play.

Between *Knights* and *Wasps* came the *Clouds*, which took
up again the theme of his earliest play of all, the *Banqueters* of
427, produced when he was possibly not yet twenty. That
theme was education, or more precisely the threat posed to
the good old moral values by the rise of a new kind of education, one that placed the premium not on knowledge and wisdom but on mere success in the world, and specifically
success in the world of democratic politics, where persua-

siveness and persuasion of mass audiences of ordinary Athenians were all-important, regardless of the inherent validity of the speaker's case.

To emblematize the New Education, Aristophanes selected Socrates, for good reasons as well as bad, and represented him as head of a Reflectory or Thinkery, a kind of institute for advanced rhetorical chicanery. In effect Aristophanes was in this way suggesting that Socrates was a Sophist, the generic brand name for this new kind of plugged-in intellectual or dangerous charlatan, according to taste.

Now, Plato (born 427), Socrates' most famous pupil or disciple, was always at pains to distance and differentiate his master from the Sophists, whom he mostly despised and execrated (a partial exception was Protagoras), on two main grounds: first, the substantive one that Socrates, unlike the Sophists, was a true master of wisdom, a genuine philosopher, whose aim was to make people's souls morally better; second, the technical ground that Socrates, unlike the Sophists, was not a professional teacher—that is, he refused to take monetary payment for his teaching.

The first of these two grounds is of course the more persuasive. Taking or not taking money was a technical distinction, and the aristocratic and snobbish Plato had a deep-seated contempt for every sort of moneymaking. But was Socrates really so categorically different from the Sophists? Were they really not philosophers at all in Plato's sense? Conversely, did Socrates have no political agenda whatsoever, no interest in influencing the kinds of arguments the masses heard and the kinds of decisions they reached?

Whether Socrates was a Sophist or not was immaterial to Aristophanes. He needed someone instantly recognizable and easily caricaturable to fill the role of Head of Reflectory, and the unattractive Socrates who wandered the streets of Athens in

ALCIBIADES

Alcibiades had grown up in the household of Pericles and Aspasia, since his father had been killed in battle when he was only a few years old. But he turned out the classic rebel without a cause—except self-promotion. Limitlessly vain, he was prepared even to turn traitor to Athens when he felt that his native city was showing him insufficient respect. Though a pupil of Socrates, he seems to have been more interested in try-ing (unsuccessfully) to seduce his teacher than in learning useful moral lessons from him.

the garb of a beggar and yet held conversations in expensive private houses both with the social elite of Athens and with distinguished visitors from abroad (such as Gorgias of Leontini in Sicily) was an obvious choice.

Twenty-four years later, though, no one would have remembered precisely what teachings Aristophanes had humorously—and inaccurately—attributed to Socrates. What they would remember, or had been told, is that Socrates' pupils included such men as the wealthy aristocrats Alcibiades and Critias: Alcibiades who had formally turned traitor to Athens in 414 (though he achieved a partial rehabilitation, he failed to deliver the goods for Athens and was murdered ignominiously in exile in 404), and Critias who had been the leader of the Thirty Tyrants *junta* in 404–3. Democracy had been restored at Athens in 403, as we have seen, but the preceding period of famine, brutal oligarchy, and civil war left a deep scar in the collective Athenian psyche, and recriminations continued for at least a generation after. When Socrates was put on trial in 399, his was just one of half-a-dozen or so major political trials of that time that represented an intense desire both to settle old scores and to wipe the slate clean of the humiliation incurred through defeat in the Peloponnesian War and the taint of internecine bloodshed. The charges against him were twofold: first, that he had committed impiety by not duly recognizing the gods the city recognized and worshiped; and, second, that he had corrupted the young through his teaching.

Bucketfuls of ink have been spilled in trying to decide whether Socrates was guilty as charged of impiety. It has even been suggested that, since his guilt on that charge was by no means manifest, the real accusation against him was the second, political one—he was really being charged with having been the teacher of Alcibiades and Critias. But that would be to underestimate the strength of the impiety charge and to misunderstand the political nature of Greek religion. Most ordinary Athenians were intensely religious in what we might call a superstitious way. Their city was a city of gods as well as men, and its prosperity depended, they thought, on establishing and maintaining right relations with the appropriate gods, above all with the city's patron Athena. A failure such as that in the Peloponnesian War, accompanied as it had been by disasters like the Great Plague of 430–426 (with a recurrence in 410), was all too easily interpreted as a token of the gods' anger. And what could more easily be thought to have provoked that anger than any signs that might be detected of impiety towards them?

Socrates apparently was to all outward appearances conventionally pious, in the sense that he performed all the usual and expected rituals. That, at any rate, was the gist of the surviving *Apology* written for Socrates by another of his disciples, Xenophon, an altogether less subtle thinker than Plato. But, as Aristophanes' *Clouds* had already hinted, and as Plato's *Apology* did nothing to contradict, Socrates' idea of the nature of the gods was very far from conventional, not at all like the everyday view held by the ordinary Athenian man-in-the-street, the type of men who formed the majority of the 501 jurors at his trial. For Socrates, a god, if truly a god, could do nothing but good, which meant discarding a great deal of Greek mythology, the Greek man or woman's popular literature.

So the religious charge, placed first and most fully developed on the charge-sheet, should be taken deadly seriously. By their own lights the jury were right to condemn Socrates as dangerously impious. The political charge, of pedagogic corruption, was added on to convince any waverers. Here before them in the dock stood the teacher of anti-democratic traitors, who was therefore himself by inference an anti-democratic

DEATH OF SOCRATES

Charles Alfonse Dufresnoy

Socrates died the death of a philosopher—so all the sources, most famously Plato in his *Phaedo*, agreed. But contrary to the impression given by Plato, and echoed here by Dufresnoy (1611–1668), death by drinking hemlock is excruciatingly painful. Yet it was preferable to the other mode of execution imposed by the Athenians on common criminals and slaves—a form of crucifixion. Socrates, in a sense, killed himself, and without the shedding of polluting blood, too. *(Galleria Palatina, Palazzo Pitti, Florence)* traitor—an inference all too simple to draw when his views on the unwisdom of the majority and such political black marks as his questionable behavior under the Thirty were, inevitably, called to the jurors' attention. A clear majority found him guilty as charged. An even larger majority voted for the death-sentence, and a few weeks later, in the most dignified way imaginable (if we are to credit Plato's brilliant *Crito* and *Phaedo* dialogues), Socrates ended his own life by a self-administered dose of hemlock.

What of his philosophy as opposed to his politics? The difficulty here is that we have not his words, but mainly Plato's and Xenophon's, often internally and mutually inconsistent. One magnificent sentence, however, from Plato's *Apology*, does echo with the ring of truth: "the unexamined life is not worth living." Socrates, it seems, was responsible for shifting the focus of intellectual inquiry away from natural philosophy (proto-scientific inquiry into the natural world and the cosmos) and political philosophy (collective, public decision-making) to the fundamental question of moral philosophy: how ought I to live? His burningly intense focus of concern was the condition of an individual person's (usually a male person's) soul.

To secure and foster the soul's health—Plato, at least, was fond of the medical analogy—Socrates sought first to know what the soul was and how it functioned. If Plato's representation of Socrates' method is accurate, Socrates was not content with any existing ordinary-language definitions of such fundamental value-terms as justice and courage. Instead, through a process of forensic question and answer, *elenchos* in Greek, he sought to get back to first principles by means of verbal deconstruction before even thinking about attempting a positive account of how to be just or courageous. Often enough the very procedure of cross-questioning contributed to an outcome of *aporia*—literally, no way to go forward. But that, in what surely was Socrates' view, was preferable to spurious claims to insight and knowledge. When told that the Delphic oracle had replied to a questioner that he, Socrates, was the wisest man on earth, he reportedly said, "Ah, yes, but that's only because I know that I know nothing (for certain)."

This was an exaggeration, of course—how could he "know" that? We recall again another famous Delphic statement, "Nothing in excess." Nevertheless, such a stance may plausibly be interpreted as marking the beginning of wisdom. And the beginning, as another sage once remarked, is half of the whole. Socrates' own life was, in a way, left sadly incomplete, like that of Jesus. But their impact on subsequent thought and behavior was probably all the greater for that.

CHAPTER 8

CYNISCA

OF SPARTA

In a dry land like Greece, for the most part lacking suitable meadow and pasture, the rearing and keeping of horses were rich men's perquisites. Chariot-racing in Greece was therefore a sheer luxury, rather than a pleasant way of preparing to fight with chariots in battle (as the Assyrians, for example, so triumphantly did). The premier event in the Greek sporting calendar was the four-horse chariot-race held at Olympia every four years. This was the race that Cynisca was the first woman to win, though she did so by proxy: as owner rather than driver. *(Le Louvre, Paris)*

Cynisca sounds like a childhood nickname, because it means (female) puppy. But it almost certainly wasn't that, as we know of adult males called by the masculine equivalent Cyniscus. Our Cynisca was, in any case, anything but puppyish in adult life. Born at Sparta probably some time around 440 B.C.E., she became the first woman ever to win a victory in the Olympic Games, a feat which she repeated at the immediately succeeding Games. But she did not have to compete in person, as we shall see.

At the probable time of Cynisca's birth, Sparta was one of the two major powers of mainland Greece, indeed of the entire Greek world. The other was democratic, naval-imperial Athens, with whom Sparta's relations since their Persian Wars entente had been strained to the point of outright military conflict during the First Peloponnesian War (460–445 B.C.E.). A sort of peace, technically a truce, had been patched up between them in 445, but that had involved Sparta's recognizing the Athenians' empire, and that smarted among an influential section of Spartans just looking for a pretext for a renewed showdown with their enemies.

141

Such a pretext had arisen, they thought, with the revolt in 441 of Samos, a strategically crucial island-city just off the Turkish coast, control of which was vital to Athens' continuing grip on its Aegean naval alliance. The siege of Samos, led by Pericles, lasted many months and was very costly both politically and financially. Leading Samian opponents of Athens had certainly appealed for help to Athens' major non-Greek rival Persia (then technically at peace with Athens); it's very likely that they also made an appeal to Sparta, likewise then technically at peace with Athens. The local Persian viceroy sent some aid. The Spartans on their part apparently called a congress of their allies, at which the issue of intervention was debated. Not for the first time they found their interventionist view opposed by the Corinthians, who argued that it would be wrong to interfere in the internal affairs of another alliance if that alliance had not directly interfered in their own sphere.

The Corinthians' view prevailed, but within a decade the boot was on the other foot. In the late 430s, the Corinthians were positively urging the Spartans to declare war on Athens and her empire, on the grounds that Athens had broken the terms of the truce of 445. The Spartans, ordinary Spartans anyway, apparently needed little persuading. Not least because they thought they would beat the Athenians easily and quickly, they voted in 432 for an all-out war. Or rather they shouted for it, because that was how voting was normally conducted in the Spartan assembly. But contrary to majority Spartan expectation, the war that began in 431 with a Spartan invasion of Athens' home territory did not end soon, and victory came anything but easily or predictably some twenty-seven years later.

That was the international background against which Cynisca was born, grew up, and attained her middle years. But Cynisca was no ordinary Spartan girl. She was a royal princess. And, if Thucydides' remarkable account of the proceedings in the Spartan assembly in 432 is to be believed, there had been at least one powerful voice raised against the notion of going to war with Athens, the voice of (probably) Cynisca's father, king Archidamus II. Nevertheless, according to the Spartan system of governance it fell to him, as the senior of the two kings, to lead the expeditionary forces against Athens, which he did until he died in 427. He was succeeded by his older son, Agis II, born to Archidamus' first wife (who was also Archidamus' aunt). But Cynisca was probably a child of her father's second marriage and so the full sister of the man who was to succeed Agis as King Agesilaus II in around 400.

Spartan royal marital relations were complex, not surprisingly, since, as in all such dynastic regimes, economic and above all political considerations were involved. But by Spartan standards they were not exceptionally complex, since the rules governing Spartan marriages were by general Greek standards simply extraordinary, if not unbelievable. Spartan girls married significantly later than their sisters elsewhere, in their late teens rather than as soon as feasible after puberty. This was supposedly for eugenic reasons, to enable them to withstand better the pangs of childbirth. But it also had the effect of narrowing both the physical and emotional gap between them and their husbands, who would typically (as elsewhere in Greece) be in their mid- to late twenties.

This relative equality between the sexes in marriage was prepared for and reinforced by giving the Spartan girls something like an equivalent to the physical part of the Spartan boys' state-run upbringing. Some very fine bronze figurines made in Sparta showing adolescent girls or young women in athletic—and literally gymnastic (i.e. naked)—poses are a powerful illustration of this social phenomenon, unique in

Greece. There is even evidence that there was a female coun-
terpart to the system of male pederastic pairing relationships
that was a required component of the educational curriculum
once a boy attained his teens. At around the time of the outbreak of the Peloponnesian War, for example, Cynisca's
brother Agesilaus became the younger beloved of Lysander,
the man who led the Spartans to eventual victory over
Athens in 404.

Marriage, however, did not preclude officially sanctioned
extramarital heterosexual relations for both partners. This
again shocked most other Greeks, who wrote Spartan girls off
as "thigh-showers" because they wore revealing mini-tunics
and considered all Spartan women little better than hussies.
But defenders of Sparta, like Xenophon (who lived in Sparta
for a while as an exile from Athens and at his patron Agesilaus's suggestion put his two sons through the official Spartan
education), looked for sociological reasons to account for
what anthropologists have called the plural marriage system
of Sparta. One powerful reason could well have been eugenic
in the sense of a concern to keep up the numbers of legitimate, especially male, Spartan births. This concern is well attested to in a number of contexts and can be explained by the
Spartans' need for constant vigilance not only against their
foreign enemies but also against their "enemy within": the
serf-like Greek population of Helots who were many times
more numerous than they.

Some of the Helots were perfectly accommodated to their
lot; those, for example, who acted as Cynisca's household ser-
vants and no doubt confidantes, who did the food- and
clothes-preparation that in other Greek cities would have
been done by citizen wives and daughters. But there were significant numbers of disaffected Helots, especially those in the
geographical region of Messenia to the west of the Taygetus

mountain range, who longed for their national independence from Sparta and had indeed risen in revolt more than once to try to get it. This constant threat was one reason for the prudent cautiousness of men like King Archidamus in not wanting to involve Sparta in unpredictable overseas adventures. The Helot threat also accounts in significant part for the existence and nature of the Spartan educational regime and for the fact that Spartan communal life resembled a soldier's life in barracks more than the normal civilian life lived in other Greek cities.

A Spartan citizen's life was not all fighting or play-fighting, however. Religion was of paramount importance to the Spartans, and line-dancing was a useful way of both honoring the gods and enhancing the communal rhythm and cohesion needed by hoplites fighting in the phalanx formation. As for the girls, they danced not only in Sparta but in a number of other towns in the vicinity. For the Hyacinthia festival, for example, held in honor of Apollo at Amyclae a few kilometers south of Sparta, girls were taken by chariot, and a passage in Xenophon's biography of Agesilaus tells of how even the king's daughter traveled down in the ordinary public chariot like any other girl. Cynisca presumably had not received any special treatment from Archidamus either.

Another form of religious celebration that appealed especially to the competitive and martial spirit of the Spartans was athletics. Our word comes from the Greek for prizes, and as early as the funeral games for Patroclus so thrillingly described in Homer's *Iliad* we can see how deeply the love of competitive athletic sports had become ingrained in Greek culture. Traditionally, the first panhellenic (all-Greek and only-Greek) athletics festival was the Olympics, established, according to the traditional chronology, in 776 B.C.E. Possibly that date should be lowered somewhat, and in any case

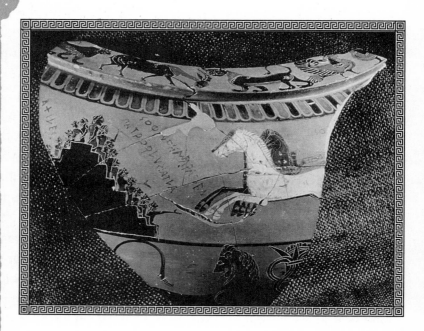

Early visual representations of scenes from Homer are rarer than you might think, but this one is as clear as one could hope for, thanks to the inscriptions. The Athenian painter has chosen to depict a scene from *Iliad* Book 23, the Funeral Games held by Achilles in honor of his dead comrade Patroclus.

"games" is a rather grand term for what was for a long time just a single running race, the equivalent of our two hundred meter sprint. But over the years other events were added, and competitors were divided into Men and Boys age categories, so that by 472, when the administration of the games was overhauled by the city of Elis that always staged them, the Olympic festival lasted five days.

The religious dimension was never forgotten. The central religious act was a procession and sacrifice to the patron god Zeus of Mt. Olympus. But the contests themselves were not conducted in what we would consider a particularly religious spirit, and many Greeks showed an ungodly determination to win at all costs and by (almost) any means. Deaths were not uncommon in the combat sports, and the competitive atmosphere made the whole thing more of a paramilitary exercise than a communal act of ritual religious worship. One reason for this was that athletics, like so many other fundamental aspects of Greek culture, was radically gendered.

The Olympics was strictly men-only, so much so that women (apart, perhaps, from an official priestess) were not even allowed to watch the men compete. A story, possibly apocryphal, went that a woman from the island of Rhodes, whose father was an Olympic victor and whose son was competing, disguised herself as a man in her eagerness to watch her son but fell over and so revealed her true sex. Greek notions of masculinity were appropriately tested at Olympia, especially in the fearsome *pankration*, a combination of judo and all-out wrestling, and in the nearly bare-knuckle boxing contests. But the premier event, partly because it was the oldest, was the two hundred meter sprint known as the *stadion* (whence our word "stadium"). The man who won this gave his name to the entire Games. Technically, though, his prize, like that of all Olympic victors, was just a token: a wreath made of olive leaves from the sacred Altis grove. But that of course was the point: an Olympic victory was in itself sufficient reward, since it was paid in the most valuable currency of all—fame. All Olympic victors were revered, after their death as well as during their lifetimes, and this is where, surprising as it may seem, Cynisca comes in.

Apart from the running events and the combat events, which took place on or around the main stadium at Olympia, there were also equestrian events which were held in a separate hippodrome (literally, a course for horses). In these alone, or more specifically in the four-horse chariot race alone, could women enter, and then by proxy, as owners of the chariots and teams, not as drivers (who were always men or boys: witness, most famously, the bronze Charioteer of Delphi, set up in commemoration of a victory at the Pythian Games, the other four-yearly panhellenic competition). And so Cynisca entered her team, in 396, and won. And again in 392, winning once more.

We know quite a lot about these two victories of hers because they caught the notice and the imagination of a much later traveler, Pausanias, who came that way about the middle of the second century c.e. Still visible and legible then was the inscription set into the base of the commemorative monument that Cynisca had had erected:

> My fathers and brothers were Spartan kings,
> I won with a team of fast-footed horses,
> and put up this monument: I am Cynisca:
> I say I am the only woman in all Greece
> to have won this wreath.

Cynisca seems not to have been shy and retiring. Or so we would have thought, had we not also possessed Xenophon's

Boxing was nothing new in Classical Greece. A
Minoan (Cretan-style) fresco of the first half of
the 2nd millennium B.C.E. from the island of
Santorini (ancient Thera) depicts two pugilists
squaring off. But it was mightily respected
there, and even had its own semi-divine patron, Polydeuces ("Pollux" in Latin). Greek
boxers did not use gloves, but bound their
hands with thongs of leather. Here, the 6th-
century Athenian artist (possibly the Nicos-
thenes who "signs" down the middle as having
"made" the vessel) has spared the viewer none
of the gory detail.

biography of her brother, written, no doubt, with Agesilaus's full knowledge and approval as a work of propaganda for publication immediately after his death (in 359). In this we learn that it was his, not his sister's, idea that she should breed chariot racehorses and compete with them at Olympia, his point being to demonstrate that such victories were won merely by wealth, unlike victories in other events and spheres (above all battle), where manly virtue was what counted decisively. Who would want a prize a woman could win (especially if she might beat you)?

In thus trying to diminish his sister's pioneering achievement and conspicuously panhellenic glory Agesilaus was cunningly playing to a longstanding strain of Greek thinking that jeered at mere athletic accomplishments (beyond the capabilities of all but a very few) and praised skills and virtues that were more widely and communally available. But lots of Greek men, including Spartans, failed to see eye to eye with Agesilaus on this, and Spartans were, for very long stretches, the single most successful national group of racehorse breeders at Olympia and elsewhere. After Cynisca's death, whenever that was, she was awarded a heroine's shrine in Sparta, and the religious veneration that entailed. Many Greek men would have given their eyeteeth for that.

CHAPTER **9**

EPAMINONDAS
OF THEBES

NEREID MONUMENT

In around 400 B.C.E. a non-Greek dynast from Xanthos in Lycia (southwest Turkey today) commissioned a tomb known as the Nereid Monument (from the representations it bears of these divine sea nymphs). He was obviously in close contact with Greek culture and society, as the scenes represented on his tomb were purely Greek. Here we see a Greek-style hoplite marching purposefully to the right. He holds his large round shield, in reality mainly made of wood, on his left arm and takes the weight by passing his arm through a shieldband and gripping a handle inside the rim. His helmet is shown tilted back off his face, either for artistic reasons or because this was the moment just before battle was engaged. These were the sort of soldiers that Epaminondas turned into the most effective fighting force in Greece. (British Museum)

E paminondas was, in the opinion of a good judge (Sir Walter Raleigh), the greatest of the ancient Greeks; this opinion carries the more weight since it was Raleigh's view that "we read Histories to inform our understanding by the examples therein found" (*History of the World*, Book 4, ch. 2.3). We today tend not to think that history's purpose, or at any rate its chief purpose, is to teach philosophy by example, but if an example did happen to be sought, like Raleigh I too would go for Epaminondas. His combination of man of action and man of reflection would have been unusual in any age. It was especially unusual in his own day, when the worlds of deed and of thought were growing rapidly apart.

We do not know Epaminondas's precise date of birth, but since he first comes to notice in the mid-380s we would probably be safe in putting it not before 415 or thereabouts. He was probably too young, therefore, to have experienced the Peloponnesian War personally as a warrior but just the right age to profit by absorbing the lessons of the experiences of his father's generation. The Peloponnesian War may have been bad news for Greece and the Greeks as a whole—that was

153

one of the loudest and clearest messages of Thucydides' history, echoed all the way down to Pausanias, the second-century c.e. traveler. But Thebes actually did rather well out of it, both economically and politically, so well, in fact, that it frightened even her senior ally Sparta (as we have seen in the previous chapter).

Thebes' importance in Greek history stems partly from its geographical situation in central Greece and more particularly from its ability to dominate for long periods the region of which it was the principal city, Boeotia. The Boeotians had a poor reputation in ancient Greece as crassly anti-intellectual gluttons, but that was largely a smear spread by their snooty near-neighbors in Athens. After all, Pindar and Plutarch, not to mention Epaminondas himself, were Boeotians. Pericles was nearer the mark when he said that the Boeotian cities were like tall oaks that crash together in a storm and act as their own executioners. Strife between the cities of Boeotia was endemic and deadly; twice in Epaminondas's lifetime Thebes dealt violently with a rival.

Yet the Boeotians of Epaminondas's day were also quite exceptionally creative in the political sphere in one main respect: their practice and sponsorship of federalism, both at home and abroad. By federalism is meant the sharing by a number of cities in a higher, federated citizenship without giving up citizenship in one's own home city or community. Thus a citizen of Thebes was also a citizen of the federal state of Boeotia. Conversely, the city of Thebes functioned also as the federation's capital, where plenary sessions of the federal council or assembly were held and the federation's central administrative offices of government were located. So too the Thebans in particular made crucial advances in military tactics during the latter part of the fifth century and, thanks above all to Epaminondas and a couple of his contemporaries, both

THUCYDIDES

Widely acknowledged as the greatest military and political historian of antiquity, and perhaps of all time, Thucydides wrote up his history of the Peloponnesian War in the belief that, should a similar set of circumstances recur, a reading of his detailed and accurate account might prove useful in either avoiding war altogether or conducting it to the best advantage. Sadly, it has far more often been useful in the latter than in the former sense. Thucydides's narrative of the battle of Delium (424 B.C.E.) foreshadows the Thebans' great military triumphs of half a century later. (*Museo Nazionale, Naples*) in tactics and in socio-military organization in the first half of the fourth. So effective were these innovations that, as we shall see, the Thebans inflicted on Sparta its first major defeat in pitched battle on land in some three hundred years. Epaminondas put this political and military creativity in the service of a crusade of liberation.

From 447 to 386 all but a couple of the twenty or so Boeotian cities were united in a federal state run on oligarchic lines; that is, power was weighted towards the richest third of Boeotian adult male citizens who could afford to equip themselves either as hoplites (heavy-armed infantrymen) or as cavalrymen. These men formed the elected local councils, which were so organized that a quarter of the members were in permanent session at any one time, each for a quarter of the year. They too were eligible to serve on the elected federal council, which was the federal state's administrative organ. This council numbered 660 and was organized on the same principle as the local councils: four groups of 165 members each served continuously for three months, while major decisions such as war or peace were taken by plenary session of the entire council. The state's executive was formed by an annually elected body of eleven Boeotarchs ("officers of the Boeotians"), whose principal sphere of authority was military command and its attendant strategic and financial responsibilities. But they could also influence policy and might impart to their deliberation and advice a definite ideological spin.

Contributions to federal finances and to the federal army were organized on the same proportional principle as contributions to membership of the federal council. Strictly, of course, it was only the interests of the wealthier Boeotians that were being equally represented at the local and federal levels of government, but nevertheless the grounding principle of the oligarchic Boeotian federal state between 447 and 386 was proportional representation. There was, however, a further qualification of this equality principle. While there were some seventeen self-administering cities at local level, they were organized for federal purposes into only eleven units or wards. This meant that some of the smaller cities found themselves under the authority—effectively under the control—of the larger ones, of which there were chiefly two: Thebes and Orchomenus, geographically separated by Lake Copais (now drained). As often in ancient Greek interstate politics, these two cities were strong rivals. The history of their rivalry during Epaminondas's lifetime is one of Orchomenus's steady eclipse and eventual obliteration by Thebes.

The foundation of this oligarchic federal state followed on the liberation of Boeotia from a decade of Athenian control and democratic intervention. It was this federal state that, as an ally of Sparta, did so well out of the Peloponnesian War. But within a decade of that war's end, thanks largely to Spartan diplomatic hamfistedness, the Boeotians (as the state was technically known) were allied with Sparta's defeated enemy Athens, with Sparta's permanent Peloponnesian enemy Argos, and with another disaffected Peloponnesian League ally, Corinth, in a quadruple alliance that had the significant financial backing of Persia (which wanted to drive Spartan garrisons and armies out of Asia). The so-called Corinthian War dragged on for almost a decade, from 395 to 386, until finally Sparta agreed to Persia's terms for withdrawal from Asia in return for Persian financial backing and a free hand in mainland Greece.

One of the immediate outcomes of the King's Peace of 386 was the dissolution of the Boeotian oligarchic federal state on the orders of King Agesilaus II of Sparta. This was not because Agesilaus had any objections to oligarchy as such. On the contrary, he was prone to impose his oligarchic cronies on all too many states. His objection to the Boeotian federal state was due to a personal blind spot about Boeotian independence. (His exiled former co-king Pausanias saw things very differently. He would even have been willing to tolerate a democracy in the Arcadian city of Mantinea, even though Mantinea had not been especially helpful to Sparta during the Corinthian War, because that was what the majority of Mantineans wanted.) Thus the major sin of intervention that Agesilaus committed during this period was at Thebes, so heinous (because sacrilegious) that even his client and future tame biographer Xenophon was moved to protest.

In 382 a Spartan force seized the acropolis of Thebes and garrisoned it, deploying their military muscle to impose on Thebes a *junta* every bit as narrowly oligarchic and unpopular as the Thirty Tyrants regime imposed by Sparta on Athens in 404. This was in flat contradiction of the autonomy clause of the King's Peace and a clear breach of the religious oath the Spartans had sworn to uphold it. The Theban *junta* lasted for three years, during which time Sparta sought to impose similar authoritarian regimes backed by garrisons throughout Boeotia.

Once more, Spartan hamfistedness threw together Athens and Thebes, and in midwinter 379–378 Thebes was liberated in rather lurid circumstances. A group of Theban national liberation fighters led by Pelopidas and supported by Athens were smuggled into Thebes in drag. They murdered the leaders of the *junta* and ousted the Spartan garrison, proclaiming not just the freedom of Thebes but the establishment of a new, moderately democratic form of government. Shortly after, these democratic Thebans, with Epaminondas as well as Pelopidas now to the fore, refounded the Boeotian federal state, on similarly moderate democratic lines, and reformed the Boeotian federal army.

Here, besides Epaminondas and Pelopidas, a key role was played also by Gorgidas, who was credited with creating the elite hoplite regiment known as the Sacred Band. The most remarkable feature of this new body was that it consisted of 150 homosexual couples. Even the Spartans had not gone so far as that, since their pairing relationships typically ended when the junior partner became an adult warrior. In command of the Sacred Band was Pelopidas, and the force was brilliantly integrated by Epaminondas on the left wing of his new-style, fifty-deep hoplite phalanx. (In previous hoplite warfare, which was for the most part extremely traditional and conservative, the crack troops had been stationed on the right wing, and the normal depth of phalanx had been just eight ranks.)

The new formation and tactics achieved their greatest triumph on the battlefield of Leuctra in Boeotia in 371 against an invading Spartan force led by King Cleombrotus. The Spartans contributed to their own demise by being unusually disorganized and demoralized, but they were beaten chiefly by Epaminondas's inspired leadership and innovative tactics and resources. Cleombrotus and some four hundred Spartans were slain. Within a few months of that catastrophe, the Spartans found their home territory of Laconia and Messenia invaded for the first time since their own ancestors had entered and conquered it over three centuries earlier.

The lasting consequence of that first invasion (in all, Epaminondas conducted four invasions of the Peloponnese during the next decade) was the independence and political reconstitution of the Messenian Helots. The adult males among them were now once again the Messenians, free citizens of the recovered *polis* of Messene. People of Messenian descent flocked back from exile as far away as north Africa and Sicily to re-establish their Messenian political identity. The city-walls of Messene that were built then still stand today in a

remarkable state of preservation as a lasting testimony to
Epaminondas's achievement. The loss of Messenia and the
Messenian Helots meant that Sparta could never again be a
great power. Epaminondas deserves to be remembered as the
great liberator of ancient Greece, alongside Themistocles.

Almost as bad for Sparta was what followed shortly after in
Arcadia, where under Epaminondas's guidance the new city of
Megalopolis arose to block Sparta's easiest route of egress by
land towards the northern Peloponnese and central Greece.
Mantinea was refortified, and, to cap it all, a new Arcadian federal state was formed with Megalopolis as its capital. Federalism, it would appear, was Epaminondas's favored solution to
the problem of interstate relations, and he apparently saw the
relationship of his Boeotia to the other Greek states not in conventional terms of imperial domination—that had been the
way of Sparta and Athens—but as a sort of super-federalism in
which Boeotia would be a first among equals in a decently proportional international system. Epaminondas, on the other
side, is to be credited personally with the extraordinarily liberated and liberationist vision that conceived that result, and
with the diplomatic and military skill required for the enormously complex and dangerous military expedition that was
needed to translate that vision into reality.

Alas, it all ended in tears, with Epaminondas's death, on
the battlefield of Mantinea in 362, in a conflict for which
Epaminondas cannot be saddled with the chief responsibility,
though he was not entirely blameless, to be sure. A combination of domestic Boeotian jealousy and the mutual rap-
prochement of Sparta and Athens caused his demise, though
his side did actually win the battle in which he was killed.
The result of that, according to Xenophon, was even more
chaos and confusion in Greece than before, but the new
cities of Messene and Megalopolis persisted triumphantly

and that must be counted an increase in the sum of human happiness. As the verses inscribed on the base of Epaminondas's funerary statue proudly, if with some pardonable exaggeration, proclaim:

> This came from my counsel:
> Sparta has cut the hair of her glory:
> Messene takes her children in:
> a wreath of the spears of Thebe[s]
> has crowned Megalopolis:
> Greece is free.

CHAPTER 10

DIOTIMA

OF MANTINEA

Most of the fine, red-figured Athenian pottery of the 5th and 4th centuries B.C.E. was made for use in the symposium, a predominantly masculine drinking party indulged in mainly by the economically better off. The vase from which this scene comes is no exception. It shows a young man, past puberty but not old enough to have grown a full beard, being served with wine by a boy. Both wear wreaths to mark the occasion. The older male reclines on a couch. He seems to be partly clothed, or at least covered, whereas the cup-bearer is shown wholly nude. The homoerotic undertones of their eye-contact are palpable. (Le Louvre, Paris)

The four women whose lives, careers, and historical impacts we have considered so far were respectively a poet, a queen, a common-law wife and reputed intellectual, and a princess. The subject of the present chapter was, as far as we know, none of these. But then, we know about Diotima only as much as Plato, the sole source for her life, wants or allows us to know. Indeed, it is even possible, though I think it unlikely (since Plato regularly used real people as characters in his philosophical dramas), that she is a fictional creation of that master of Greek prose literature. This chapter is written on the assumption that she is not.

What is most striking about her, therefore, is precisely her gender: the fact that she was a woman. For Plato, in the remarkable dialogue known as the *Symposium,* introduces her in the context of what was otherwise an exclusively male and very masculine gathering, since a *symposion* in its original ancient Greek sense was typically convened for the louche practical purposes of wine-drinking accompanied by inebriated sex rather than for hard philosophical thinking and eloquent speechifying on the deeper meanings of Love. Moreover, Plato treats Diotima and her views with the utmost respect. As we shall see, he even gives her what is probably the "star" speech of the entire dialogue. Certainly, it is the most unorthodox and therefore the most memorable.

ENOUGH HAS BEEN SAID ALREADY, perhaps more than enough, to emphasize the point that Greek women, even free women of citizen status who were the mothers or wives of citizens, were at best second-class citizens in terms of their public role and recognition. Aristotle's philosophical conception of women was perhaps unduly negative and Plato's—to which we shall return below—was exceptionally positive, but not even Plato would have seriously considered, let alone advocated, the practical implementation at Athens or any other Greek city of feminism in its dictionary sense: that is, the according of equal treatment and status to women on the grounds that they are in all salient respects the equals of men. In one sphere of ancient Greek public life, however, women did come nearer to achieving equality than in any other, and this sphere was hardly an unimportant one. It was the sphere of religion.

The ancient Greeks, unlike some modern religions, had no problem with either the idea or the practice of women priests. Indeed, in a sense the chief priest of fifth- and fourth-century Athens—not the same as the chief religious official, who was the annual "King" Archon—was a woman: the priestess of Athena Polias (City-protecting Athena). This woman's appointment, oddly in an egalitarian democracy, was arranged on a hereditary basis from within a single aristocratic descent-group. At the time of Aristophanes' play *Lysistrata*, 411 B.C.E., Athena Polias's priestess was called Lysimache; it is almost certain that the invented name "Lysistrata" was a deliberate pun on the name of the real Lysimache, and that the audience

LYSISTRATA

Illustration. Aubrey Beardsley

Lysistrata is the fictional character who domi-
nates Aristophanes' 411 B.C.E. comic play *Lysistrata*. Aubrey Beardsley, at the height (or depth)
of late Victorian decadence, engraved a suite of
more or less pornographic images inspired by
the play. Here, Lysistrata harangues her reluctant
co-revolutionaries. Beardsley was influenced by
Japanese printmaking but also by Athenian erotic
vasepainting—the gesture towards her companion's pubic area that is being made by the
woman with what looks like a halo on her head
is a clear echo of a well-known Athenian scene.
(Victoria and Albert Museum, London)

Women priests were not a problem for the ancient Greeks. On this relief, a sheep is shown being sacrificed to Demeter by a family group, with Demeter herself represented in the form of a priestess on the right. Blood sacrifices such as these helped to bind human communities together while at the same time marking their respectful distance from and inferiority to the immortal gods, who have appropriately been called "larger Greeks." *(CM Dixon)*

was expected to recognize it as such, on account of her exceptionally high public profile.

Apart from women-priests—for female gods, of course—there were also a number of women-only festivals. The most widely attested throughout the Greek world was the Thesmophoria in honor of Demeter Thesmophoros (Law-bearing Demeter). Demeter the earth-mother goddess, who spent part of each year underground to be with her daughter Persephone, stood for the powers of fertility, animal and vegetable as well as human. That women alone, and more precisely married women, were permitted by the men to conduct such a fundamental annual ritual on behalf of the city as a whole is testimony to the awe men felt in the face of female powers of reproduction, passive but indispensable. But even that could not stop Aristophanes having a laugh at its expense, in his *Thesmophoriazusae* (*Women Celebrating the Thesmophoria*), produced in the same year as his *Lysistrata*.

The plots of the two plays reveal, in reverse, something of the true nature of gender-relations and mutual gender-perceptions in late-fifth-century Athens and probably most of the rest of Greece, with the possible exception of Sparta. In the *Lysistrata*, citizen wives from both sides of the Peloponnesian War conflict conspire to put a stop to the war, since their husbands clearly have neither the will nor the means to do so by themselves. Their method of bringing them kicking and screaming to the negotiating table is simple (and not without documented counterparts in historical actuality): a collective sex-strike. But to make doubly sure of male compliance, the women conspirators also seize the Acropolis of Athens where the state treasury is housed (in the Parthenon). The plot is ultimately successful.

The plot of the *Thesmophoriazusae* has certain similarities but is at the same time more complex and more parochial.

Again, a conspiracy of women is involved, hatched earlier at another women-only fertility festival, the Skira. The context in which the plot (in more than one sense) is developed on stage is the festival that gives the play its name, the Thesmophoria. At this celebration the women plan to kill the tragic playwright Euripides for his unflattering portraits of women in his plays, and, more especially, for revealing their secret: that they are all congenitally and uncontrollably mad for drink and sex. Euripides gets to hear of this plot because the Thesmophoria has been infiltrated by a man in drag (surely the realization of a genuine Athenian male fantasy), a relative of his. The rest of the play involves the comic unmasking of the relative and the pursuit of the unfortunate Euripides.

But neither comedy, be it noted, satirizes or otherwise makes fun of women's roles in civic religion as such. That would have been too close to the knuckle. On the other hand, not all religious practices were considered equally important, valid, or sacrosanct, and Greek men regularly believed—indeed, they probably had the idea dinned into them from an early age—that women were more predisposed to the wilder and more emotional sorts of religious display than they were themselves. Consider most obviously the mythical Bacchae or Maenads (literally "madwomen") who were the special devotees of the patron god of drama, Dionysus. In the plot of the play by Euripides that is named after them, the *Bacchae* of 406, a mother in her frenzied ecstasy mistakes her son for a wild animal and actually tears apart his living body—offstage, of course. Women thus came to be thought of as models for possession, whether by Dionysus, as in this unfortunate case, or by Apollo, as in the case of the more controlled outpourings of the oracular priestess at Delphi.

With such possession, or divinely inspired madness, might come either a unique and beneficial insight or a terrible destructiveness. It was all rather unpredictable, as were women themselves, or so men seem to have thought. But the men were not so sexist as to refuse to take advantage of any religious insight that a woman might possibly have, especially if that could be turned to communal good. Such was the case of our Diotima. Or rather of Plato's Diotima, since she is not attested to outside the pages of his *Symposium*. As she is represented there, she was a woman of Mantinea whom Socrates somehow and somewhere met, an expert on the subject of love—that is, erotic passion—as well as on a number of other matters. For example, Socrates says, "on one occasion when the Athenians performed their sacrificial rites to ward off the plague, she delayed the onset of the disease for ten years."

If literally true, that almost magical intervention would have happened in about 440, since the Great Plague struck Athens in 430, and Diotima would have been an example of the itinerant *mantis* or seer of whom we hear in Herodotus and other fifth-century sources. It is on the other hand possible to interpret Diotima as a purely fictional invention of Plato, as many scholars have done. Then, her alleged name and place of origin, although they are in themselves perfectly plausible historically, might be interpreted correspondingly as Aristophanic "speaking" names: Diotima means either "Zeus-honoring" or "Zeus-honored," and Mantinea would be a pun on *mantis*.

There would have been nothing in itself odd in Socrates' reporting the religious wisdom and insight of a woman. What is odd, however, and deliberately so, is the climactic role that Plato gives to the contributions of Diotima to the unfolding of the mini-drama that is his *Symposium*. As more than one modern critic has asked, why, indeed, is Diotima a woman? Why did Plato accord such weight to the ideas of a woman?

As we have already noted, Plato did find a place for a few exceptionally intelligent women in the ideal state of his *Re-*

Apart from drink and sex, a major delight of the Greek symposium was music. This might be supplied by the invitees themselves, or, as here, it might be supplied by buying in professional women flautists, who were often slave prostitutes. *(Museo Nazionale, Naples)*

public, not as rulers themselves but as the mates, in the sexual sense, of those equally exceptionally intelligent men. He is also reported as having had in real life a few female pupils at his Academy in Athens. However, that is very far from making Plato a feminist. Rather, it was something about the subject in hand, and something about the philosophical spin that he wanted to give it, that made it seem appropriate for him to use a woman as his crucial mouthpiece.

THE TOPIC OF THE *Symposium*, broadly speaking, was *eros*, which in everyday Greek language normally connoted strong sexual desire rather than some more generalized feeling of affection, even deep affection (for which the Greek was *philia*). It was also, of course, the name of the male god who symbolically represented that kind of human desire. The discussion of *eros* (reported at several removes, a mark of Plato's usual art and artifice) took place at Agathon's, that is at the house of the tragic playwright Agathon, who had held a very special drinking party to celebrate his first victory at a state drama-festival in 416 B.C.E. That, then, is the supposed original dialogue's dramatic date. Plato actually wrote his version of it several (at least three) decades later.

Agathon's dining room or *andron* (literally, the room for men) probably had the standard number of seven couches on which his guests reclined. They included Phaedrus, Pausanias (Agathon's beloved in real life), Eryximachus (a doctor), and Aristophanes, each of whom, prompted by Socrates, gave a set speech. Agathon himself also spoke formally. Socrates, penultimately, introduced a version of a dialogue he had had with Diotima, together with a reported set speech of hers. Finally, in a sort of Aristophanic comic coda, a very drunken Alcibiades bursts in on the proceedings towards the end and delivers his set speech.

Socrates uses Diotima as a device both for indicating the deficiencies, in his (and Plato's) view, of the conceptions of the previous speakers and to enunciate a positive doctrine (which Alcibiades in effect confirms). Against a background of homoerotic love, which both is pedagogically realistic and suits the thrust of Diotima's argument, she claims that love's desire is for immortality through procreation. These offspring of mental "pregnancy" include above all virtuous acts, educational discussions, works of art, and legislation. Ultimately, as she puts it, the intercourse between a (Platonic) philosopher and perfect beauty issues in the birth of true virtue.

Thus the narrowly sexual dimension of *eros*, which in mundane reality was the dominant dimension for most ordinary Greeks, is here filtered out by Diotima to leave only the pure deposit of the metaphorical love of beauty. Whether, as has been argued, that is a particularly feminine way of looking at the relationship between philosophy, beauty, and true virtue is another matter. All that we may assert for certain is that in choosing a woman as his indirect mouthpiece Plato was signaling very loudly that the doctrine being enunciated was pretty radically unorthodox.

If we turn from the heights of the *Symposium* to the first book of the *Politics* by Plato's pupil, Aristotle, we find ourselves back in the realm of soberly realistic conventionality once again. For here we find it stated dogmatically that woman by definition, Aristotle's definition, is by nature an incomplete male, and that one of the telltale stigmata of that unalterably inferior nature is her lack of rational capacity. There is no room for a Diotima in Aristotle's ideal city, or in the real Mantinea of either the fifth or the fourth century.

CHAPTER 11

PASION

OF SYRIA AND ATHENS

Only three scenes survive on pots of shoemakers at work. Shoemaking was a relatively respectable craft, practiced by citizens, though the more successful of them would also employ slave assistants. One, a man called Simon, is even presented in a dialogue of Plato as engaging in serious conversation with Socrates. Here, a shoemaker cuts out leather around the sole of a customer who stands on a table. *(Ashmolean Museum, Oxford)*

In Aristotle's worldview women, even free women, sat uncomfortably close to slaves. A woman's natural inability to reason effectively rendered her something akin to a natural slave, who could not reason at all and required the reason of a master to enable him or her to function usefully in society. Aristotle's doctrine of natural slavery may be repellent to us today, but it was authorized, in a sense, by the fact that the Greek world was one that did not just have slaves but one that was unthinkable without them. It was a slave society, or rather a collection of often very different slave societies (compare and contrast Athens and Sparta, for conspicuous instance). Greek civilization, to put it another way, rested on slavery.

During the fifth century B.C.E. many hundreds of thousands of men and women, girls and boys entered the Greek world from their native "barbarian" countries as slaves: that is, as chattels, commodities, items of trade purveyed by specialist slave traders using specialized slave markets. Their purchasers were mainly Greek citizens, but also Greeks who were resident aliens of a city other than the one where they

177

held citizenship (a very common situation at Athens, as we shall see) and non-Greeks resident in a Greek city (again, Athens was a frequent example). The most common generic name for slaves was *doulos*, but there were altogether a dozen Greek words meaning "slave," a sure indication of both the widespread character of the institution and the gradations of status to be found among the unfree. A rather unpleasant naming practice, common in other slave societies as well (for example, in the American Old South), was to refer to a slave as a *pais*, literally a child (male or female), even when the slave was a fully grown adult; compare the American "boy."

In one respect, the Greeks' practice of slavery was original. Slavery of various sorts is found from the very beginning of human civilization. But the Greeks were the first to create the slave in the complete sense, what is sometimes called the chattel slave: that is, an unfree person who has been alienated forcibly from his or her natal family and community, traded as a mere commodity, and kept as property without any effective personal, let alone political, rights. It has been well noted that the development of chattel slavery was carried furthest in the city which boasted the achievement of the greatest degree of both personal and political liberty, at any rate for adult male citizens, namely democratic Athens. This was not merely a coincidence. The freedom of the democratic Athenian citizen was both achieved at the expense of, and acquired its special symbolic meaning from, the exploitation of many thousands of chattel slaves.

Just how many slaves there were in Classical Greece at any one time is unknown and unknowable. We cannot even say for sure how many there might have been in, say, Athens in 400 B.C.E. The Greeks did not keep the relevant sorts of statistics, and their historians displayed a corresponding disinterest in anything like the precision a modern historian would ideally demand. But there are figures preserved, not all of which are demonstrably fantastic. One that is just that, however, is the four hundred thousand slaves registered in a military census taken in Athens and Attica in the 310s. Apart from the gross disproportion that would have entailed between the slave and the free populations, it would have meant a total population of half a million or more, which simply could not have been sustained by the carrying capacity of Attica even when eked out by imports of necessities.

Modern estimates of Athens' total population, and of its breakdown between slave and citizen, are more reasonable. The largest population achieved, during the second half of the fifth century, before the losses of the Peloponnesian War, would have been of the order of 250,000 to 300,000. Of these, slaves probably constituted no more than one third, in absolute terms numbering perhaps 80,000 to 100,000. The resident free population was divided between citizen families and resident aliens. The latter may have reached a maximum of 50,000, leaving the adult male citizens and their families to account for something like 100,000 to 150,000.

In a slave society one way of asserting and corroborating one's own sense of personal worth and identity is to own other human beings as slaves. Other things being equal, it is safe to say that, if it was financially viable, slave-ownership would be sought; sometimes Greeks bought a slave even when, on strict economic grounds, it did not make sense to do so. Rich people, of course, were in a much better position to do so than the poor. One ancient Greek definition of freedom was not having to be dependent on anyone else; conversely, unfreedom was having to depend on another for one's livelihood and lifestyle.

So rich Greeks bought slaves to keep them in the leisured comfort and luxury they desired. Lower down the scale, even

THE AGORA

This imaginary representation shows a scene
from the ancient Athenian Agora or Market-
place-cum-Civic Center. The Agora was formally defined about the time of Solon and by
the time of Pasion it had come to be marked
out into distinct areas: the bankers, the per-
fumers, the flower-sellers, and so forth. But together with these commercial activities, within
the same general space, were conducted such
fundamental civic activities as the hearing of
lawsuits by the People's court. *(Mary Evans Picture Library)*

a fairly humble peasant farmer might be in a position to own at least a single household slave, both to help him out on the land and to act as a household servant for his wife and family. Wealthier farmers, who nevertheless had to work for a living, would own several slaves, one of whom in times of war would serve as their personal batman on campaign while the others were left behind to mind the farm.

Not everyone was engaged exclusively in the agricultural sector, though that perhaps occupied 90 percent of the workforce of a typical Greek city. Craftsmen of various sorts were required, especially metalworkers and pottery-makers, and when production reached any sort of size, slave assistants were invariably purchased and trained up. Some slave-craftsmen were given the privilege of working apart from their masters, without direct supervision, in return for the payment of a fixed percentage of the proceeds of the sale of their products. Traders in both staples and luxury goods were of two sorts, the local retail traders and hucksters, and the long-distance seagoing merchants. Slaves were employed as the former by the latter. And as the business of trade and commerce became more complex and specialized during the fifth century, a particular type of slave emerged, the slave banker. Our Pasion belonged to this last, exceptional world.

Then there was a class of work that was almost a slave monopoly, namely mining. The most famous instance was the mining of silver-bearing lead at Laurium in southeast Attica, where the remains of the worked-out shafts can still be seen. Slave miners were the lowest of the low. They were worked literally to death, which presumably came as a happy release for many. At their peak the Laurium mines employed somewhere between ten and thirty thousand slave workers. Citizen plutocrats might lease out their slaves to other concessionaires in these state-owned mines: we hear, for example, that the well-known general Nicias drew income from no fewer than one thousand of these, the rental of whom was handled by a freedman (manumitted ex-slave) of his.

Finally, at the opposite end of the social spectrum from the mine slaves, there were the public slaves, slaves owned by a community collectively rather than by an individual master or mistress. Such were the Scythian archers at Athens who fulfilled some of the functions of a police force, including the arrest of citizens. Such too were the various scribal functionaries who enabled the bureaucracy of Athenian government to proceed on a daily basis by keeping records of laws, decrees, and court-decisions, by supervising the exchange of coins in the marketplace in the Piraeus, and so on. Pasion, though privately owned, approximated in status far more closely to these privileged public slaves than to the appallingly maltreated mine-slaves.

WE DO NOT KNOW EXACTLY WHERE Pasion was from nor when he came to Athens, and Pasion, presumably, was not his natal name. He may have been originally Syrian from the Levant and, since he died when elderly in 370 or 369, he perhaps arrived in the Athens slave-market as a boy somewhere around 440 B.C.E., shortly after peace with Persia would have made fresh supplies of such Syrian slaves available to Greek slave traders through the Phoenician ports of Tyre and Sidon. (In the sixth century the flow of slave trade had been the other way, as we learn from *Ezekiel* 27.13 [RSV translation]: "Javan, Tubal, and Meshech traded with you; they exchanged the persons of men and vessels of bronze for your merchandise"—Javan, derived from the Greek ethnic "Ionians," was the Hebrew for "Greeks.") We do, however, know who bought Pasion, as we know a number of other things about his personal life, from a series of preserved Athenian courtroom speeches.

Litigation, as Aristophanes' comedy *Wasps* (422 B.C.E.) makes abundantly plain, was a central aspect of the Athenian democracy. The Athenian People ruled in the courts as they did in the Assembly, and the courts were the scene of any number of high-profile political trials. Athens, as center of an empire, was also an unusually large, complex, and heterogeneous society, in which the scope for clashes that might end in court was enormous. Of this original flood we get access to only a small trickle of cases involving litigants who had the wealth and the pressing concern to hire the very best speechwriters, such as Isocrates and Demosthenes, who might then publish a version of the speeches their clients had actually delivered in the trial itself. Such a one was Isocrates' speech seventeen, delivered on behalf of an unnamed young man of high social position at Panticapaeum in what is now the Crimea, on the northern shore of the Black Sea. This young man had a quarrel, a very big quarrel indeed in purely financial terms, with Pasion.

Pasion, a slave purchased to run his Athenian master's bank, was supremely successful at his job and by this time had been liberated and granted the status of resident alien or *metic* that went automatically to such freed slaves: better than being a slave, no doubt, but very much less desirable than being an Athenian citizen. Banks at Athens—technically trapezite banks (so-called for the bankers' tables)—had begun as glorified moneychanging operations, a highly necessary function, as there were several systems of coinage involving different metals and weight-standards in use in the east Mediterranean. They were especially necessary in Athens' port city of Piraeus, where Pasion's bank was, since Piraeus had become the premier port of the entire east Mediterranean region. Hence Pasion was recommended to the young man of Isocrates' speech as someone who would aid him, a foreigner, in his business ventures at Athens.

Gradually, in addition to changing money, bankers at Athens became deposit-bankers. They accepted deposits of funds from clients, which they guaranteed to keep safe and return on request. Meanwhile, with the funds currently at their disposal, they made loans to other clients, both purely commercial and, in the case of bankers like Pasion with important connections, political. The prime type of economic loan was what is sometimes called a bottomry bond or shipping loan. A shipowner or long-distance trader might be loaned a large sum of money in order either to buy a cargo or to rent space on another man's trading ship. Strict laws governed long-distance trade and traders at Athens, often involving lawsuits, and from these we learn that, though the profits could be great, the risks of such sea ventures were also terrifically high. Bad weather, piracy, and war were constant hazards. The rates of interest charged for such shipping loans were thus extremely high, inflated further by one of such loans' regular conditions: if the cargo was lost, the loan—both principal and interest—was immediately canceled. How was one to be sure that the borrower hadn't merely pretended to have lost his cargo, for example?

The rights and wrongs of Pasion's quarrel with the unnamed prosecutor need not detain us, since the outcome of the trial (held in about 394) is unknown. What matters is that it did not in any way impede Pasion's steady rise through the economic, social, and, ultimately, political scales. Not that this rise, which looks remarkably like an ancient Greek equivalent of realizing the "American dream," could have been predicted. Clearly, Pasion was an utterly exceptional individual, who had the wit and the good fortune to profit uniquely from exceptionally fluid times.

He began his rise by inheriting from his former masters not only the bank but apparently also a wife, Archippe (despite her name's aristocratic ring, she may very well have been an

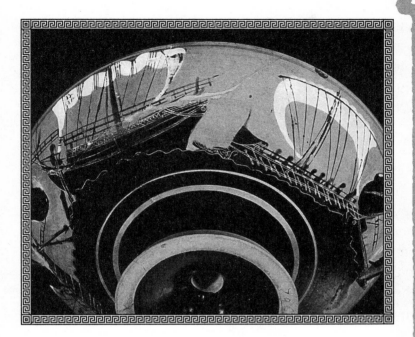

In Homer there was no distinction drawn between a warship and a purpose-built trading vessel. Homeric ships were probably imagined as being something like the small warship or pinnace depicted on the right of this fine 6th-century B.C.E. Athenian drinking cup. By the middle of the 6th century specialist merchantmen had been devised, sail-powered rather than oar-driven, and rounded rather than narrowly sleek. Greeks needed regularly to import above all metals and slaves, and, all too often, emergency food supplies too. *(Michael Holford/British Museum)*

ex-slave like Pasion himself). His goodwill remained buoy-
ant. On the strength of it he diversified into manufacture,
specifically arms-manufacture; that is, he bought skilled
craftsmen-slaves who made shields. Again, this business too
prospered, preparing the way for Pasion to take an unprecedented step across the high barrier dividing slave and *metic*
status from citizen status.

When Athens was in military difficulties, Pasion made the
city a gift of shields. Thanks to this, and thanks to his connections at the very top of Athenian political society with men like
the financial expert Callistratus and Timotheus, the son of the
war-hero Conon (honored with a portrait-statue set up at public expense in the Agora or civic center), Pasion was granted
Athenian citizenship by special public vote of the Assembly.
From entry into Athens as a chattel slave he had thus risen to
join the citizen elite. Not only was he the first to do so, but he
is the only man known to have done so apart from one of his
own ex-slaves, Phormion.

The city's then-unique grant extended to Pasion's two sons
with Archippe as well as to Pasion himself. It did not, however,
apparently include Archippe, since she seems never to have
been rated of citizen status. This together with her remarriage
(to the aforementioned Phormion) rankled enormously with
the elder of her two sons, Apollodorus, as we shall see.

CHAPTER 12

NEAERA

OF CORINTH AND ATHENS

Heterosexual eroticism was depicted no less freely in Athenian vasepainting than homosexual. Here a male figure in the background presses his attentions on a glamorously clothed young woman. He holds, or rather balances elegantly in his left hand, a drinking cup, while she carries a lyre—perhaps, therefore, she was a professional courtesan, and the couple are stealing away from a symposium to carry on their relationship in greater privacy elsewhere. (Le Louvre, Paris)

Apollodorus son of Pasion was of—at best—mixed descent, part slave, part free, part Greek, part non-Greek, in a city where citizenship depended on legitimate birth to two legally married Athenian citizen parents, and where Athenianness was highly cultivated and prized. Not surprisingly, perhaps, he grew up to be paranoid about his origins yet constantly putting himself into extremely public situations where slurs on those origins were almost bound to be expressed. One of these was a *cause célèbre* in the late 340s involving our Neaera.

We know about Apollodorus mainly because of a series of seven speeches that are preserved in the corpus attributed to Demosthenes, but which in fact were almost certainly written by Apollodorus himself. (Although he received plenty of sage advice from the great speechwriter and democratic politician, Apollodorus was not always wise enough to take it.) At any rate, his Attic prose style is often as rough as his in-your-face political style, which fits all too closely the unflattering stereotype of the typical demagogue so skillfully drawn in Plato's *Republic*.

Like Demosthenes, who was the supreme demagogue—
that is, People's leader—of his day, Apollodorus was a rich
young man without a family tradition of political prominence
who spent a good deal of his adult life involved in a massive
lawsuit involving his inheritance. Not only had his mother remarried after the death of his father, often a cause of resent-
ment in a sensitive son, but she had also remarried, to
Apollodorus's eyes, well beneath her. The new stepfather,
Phormion, to make matters even worse, was a man whose
career uncannily echoed that of Apollodorus's natural father,
Pasion. A non-Greek who apparently never lost his foreign
accent, Phormion had actually been Pasion's slave, and just
like Pasion himself when he was young, he had been freed by
Pasion as a reward for his excellence in the day-to-day management of his bank. On top of that, when Pasion died, he be-
queathed to Phormion by will both the ownership of the bank
and the potential ownership of, that is marriage to, Pasion's
widow—Apollodorus's mother. A couple of years after Pasion's death, in Apollodorus's absence from Athens, they married and soon had a new family of half-siblings.

Like others in his position, Apollodorus sought to overcom-
pensate for his feelings of insecurity and inadequacy regard-
ing his origins by being more Athenian than the Athenians. If
rich Athenian citizens were expected to dig deep into their
pockets to fund a variety of public ventures, then Apollodorus
would dig deeper than the average rich Athenian (who in fact
was often less than happily forthcoming with his contributions, as Demosthenes frequently complained). If aspiring
Athenian politicians sought to advance their careers by well-
timed and well-publicized lawsuits in which their prominent
opponents would be cast as public enemy no. 1 and they
themselves as the single-handed saviors of Athens, then
Apollodorus would take on all sorts of opponents, at once, no

matter how well- (or ill-) timed the proceedings, however good (or bad) the cause, or how prominent the opponent.

Apollodorus thus condemned himself as much as he was condemned by his background and opponents to remaining a politician of the second rank, although that in no way lessens the interest of his career to us. For example, the lawsuit he launched against Polycles in about 360 sheds light on the condition of the Athenian navy at a low ebb of Athens' fortunes preceding its defeat in the Social War of 357–355.

The Athenian empire of the fifth century had been brought down by a combination of Sparta and Persia in the Peloponnesian War. Revival began in the late 390s, but was halted again by the King's Peace of 386. In 378, however, exactly a century after the first, Athens founded a second naval alliance, this time on an explicitly anti-Spartan as opposed to anti-Persian ticket. The new League prospered remarkably, thanks to the financial acumen of Callistratus and the admiralship of Timotheus, both associates of Apollodorus's father. Some seventy-five cities quickly joined up, encouraged by the prospectus in which the Athenians swore to avoid or to actively punish the sort of Athenian behavior that had attracted allied opprobrium in their previous empire, especially by occupying or otherwise exploiting the territories of their allies.

But within twenty years, despite the best of announced intentions, Athens seemed far more interested in pursuing its own selfish agendas than in securing the interests and wishes of individual allies and of the alliance as a whole. A key figure in instigating a major allied revolt in 357 was Mausolus, the satrap of the Persian province of Caria. He was a native Carian, but considerably Hellenized culturally, and well placed to exploit the grievances of such Athenian allies as Rhodes for his own purposes, which were to get the Athenians off his back or at any rate out of his backyard in the eastern Aegean. The revolt was all too successful for the Athenians' taste, and though the Second Athenian Sea League formally remained in existence until 338, when it was disbanded at the behest of Philip of Macedon, its days of effective power and influence were over. Apollodorus's lawsuit against Polycles can been seen in retrospect as an unhappy augury of that likely outcome.

One of the obligations of rich Athenians, especially the richest four hundred or so, was to pay for the upkeep and serviceability of Athenian trireme warships. This form of taxation was pretty carefully organized and legally sanctioned. Technically, the rich donors were also supposed to captain the ships—that is what "trierarch" means—but in practice most delegated that task to a professional. Not so Apollodorus: in 362, when the Athenians were campaigning around the Hellespont (Dardanelles), partly to protect the route of their own wheat supply from the Crimea and Ukraine, he captained in person. Since public funds to pay sailors had run low or out, he paid his crews out of his own pocket besides making sure that the state-provided equipment (oars, poles) and the fabric of the ship itself were in good sailing trim. He did all this so successfully that his ship was chosen to be the admiral's flagship. But when the time came for Polycles to succeed him in command of the ship, he failed to show up; the same happened the next year, so that in all Apollodorus kept up his command and payments for more than double the officially imposed time limit. One suspects that he was not altogether downhearted to have been given this golden opportunity to parade his civic-mindedness before an Athenian popular jury.

Whether he won his case, we do not, as usual, know. He pursued thereafter a career as a minor politician broadly on the Demosthenic side from the early 340s on. In the late 340s, perhaps in frustration at his lack of success with (overcoming

The greatest oracular center of ancient Greece was Delphi, sacred to Apollo. But not far behind in importance came Dodona in northwest Greece, sacred to Apollo's father Zeus. Here several methods of divination were practiced, including divining from the rustling of oak leaves and the cooing of the sacred doves. But this inscribed lead tablet reveals yet a third method, the direct question to Zeus: "Hermon asks to which god he should pray in order to have useful children from his wife Cretaia, apart from those he already has." The message was written *boustrophedon*, "as the ox plows," that is, from left to right and right to left alternately. The question reveals the overriding function of Greek marriage as the means of legitimate procreation. *(CM Dixon)*

or persuading) men, he took on a woman, prosecuting Neaera
on the very serious public charge of impersonating a citizen.

FORMALLY, THE PROSECUTION OF Neaera was brought not by
Apollodorus but by his brother-in-law, but after speaking the
opening Theomnestos apparently handed over without ado to
Apollodorus, who delivered the main attack as supporting
speaker. It was a common practice and perfectly legal to call
supporting speakers, but this—typical of Apollodorus—was an
extreme use of the tactic. The real target of attack, however,
was in any case not Neaera herself but a rival and equally
minor politician called Stephanus, with whom Neaera shared
a household and a relationship. The aim of Apollodorus's prosecution was to undermine Stephanus indirectly by proving to
the court's satisfaction that the relationship was illegal.
Neaera, he charged, was not really Stephanus's lawfully wedded wife, because as a foreigner she was not legally qualified
to be so. Nor was Neaera, as Apollodorus represented her, dis-
qualified merely by her birth from being an Athenian wife, but
also by her whole manner of life since adolescence.

It was a usual procedure for an Athenian prosecutor not to
confine himself to the precise charge being heard but rather to
involve or drag in the whole career or lifestyle of the defendant
as an integral part of his case. This was perfectly understand-
able from a democratic Athenian point of view, since trial by
popular jury was a key part of practicing democracy, and it was
the interests of the people of Athens that any one jury was out
to protect, regardless of strict legality or even equity. Thus,
Neaera had to be shown up by Apollodorus as not merely a
bad woman breaking the law with the full connivance of the
equally bad or worse Stephanus, but as a mortal danger to the
continued health of the Athenian city insofar as that depended
on orthodox and legal Athenian marital relations.

And shown up she was, in spades, though there is no way of knowing how much of the mud heaped on the poor woman was actually true. According to the Apollodorus version of her life, anyway, Neaera began her career—in the professional sense—as a prostitute in Corinth. Even if untrue, this was a plausible detail. Pindar had referred coyly a century earlier to the "daughters of Persuasion" who plied their trade in Corinth for the benefit of passing sailors, and it was presumably an excellent place for an ambitious prostitute to serve her apprenticeship, as Neaera allegedly did, in a fairly upmarket whorehouse. From there she was "liberated" by two Athenians. That is, according to Apollodorus, Neaera had actually been a slave sex-worker and was bought into freedom by two of her clients. This story recalls the tale, told brilliantly by Herodotus, of Sappho's brother, who allegedly fell head over heels for a Thracian prostitute with the working name Rhodopis ("Rosy-cheeks") at another international entrepôt, Naucratis in Egypt, and bought her freedom.

Freedom for Neaera, however, did not mean respectability but rather a continuation of her career of prostitution in Athens. This was how she allegedly "met" Stephanus, who then (according to Apollodorus) so far from making an honest woman of her not only lived with her but made her sexual services available to others for a handsome fee.

In itself, presumably, Neaera's function as a prostitute would not have been found particularly shocking by the jury. What may have shocked them, and certainly this was Apollodorus's intention, was that Neaera's daughter, not by Stephanus and so possibly born when Neaera was still a slave prostitute in Corinth, had been married successively to two Athenian citizens, one of whom had been appointed to the chief religious office of the Athenian state, that of "king" Archon.

In death at least, if not always in life, Athenian women were treated with the very greatest of respect. Here the deceased wife or daughter is seated, in thoroughly respectable garb, and grasps the right hand of her former lord and master (either father or, more likely, husband) in a moving gesture of farewell. Death in childbed was by no means a rarity in those times. The couple's daughter, or perhaps a female slave, is shown between the two. *(Staatliche Museen, Berlin/Bildarchiv preussischer kulturbesitz)*

In other words, not only had Neaera and Stephanus broken the law twice, in illegally marrying off a woman who was not an Athenian to Athenian citizens, but the consequence of their illegal action had been public sacrilege potentially endangering the continued prosperity of the entire Athenian community. For apart from overseeing such public religious celebrations as the Lenaea festival of Dionysus (one of the two annual drama festivals), the "king" Archon also conducted an apparently archaic and secret ritual with his wife, presumably an act of sexual intercourse, during the Anthesteria festival inside a building in the Agora known quaintly as the "Oxherd's hut." Neaera's daughter, Phano, had thus polluted the very core of the Athenian *polis*, and Apollodorus was careful to name and shame her, since mentioning the name of a genuine Athenian woman in the company of unrelated men was considered the height of disrespect.

In case the jury still weren't sufficiently shocked to vote for Neaera's condemnation, Apollodorus reminded them as forcefully as he could of the significance and unique importance of the married estate. With more rhetorical artifice than literal truth (though he has too often deceived modern scholars, his original audience were presumably more clued in) he thundered: "*Hetairai* (courtesans) we have for the sake of sexual gratification, *pallakai* (concubines) in order to take care of our bodies and look after us when we are ill, but lawfully wedded wives we have for the sake of producing legitimate children and to be faithful guardians of our property at home." Actually, most of the jury could not have afforded a *hetaira*, the sort of woman Aspasia and Neaera were alleged to be, and they probably had no need of or wish for a *pallake* as well as or instead of a wife. The rhetorical emphasis belonged entirely to the third and last mentioned member of this tricolon: the lawfully wedded wife. She, according to the law of Pericles of 451 which had been re-enacted in 403, had to be not only free and legitimate herself but also an Athenian, as Neaera allegedly was not.

Neaera, being a mere woman, whether Athenian or not, could not reply to all these foul charges *in propria persona*. Women might be present in an Athenian courtroom, but they could not actually speak from the rostrum, either as prosecutors or as defendants on their own account. So the last words would have gone to Stephanus and any supporting male speakers he could muster. Sadly, they are lost to us, and we do not know the jury's verdict. But Neaera's life—or imagined life—remains of enormous importance to us as representing women's two-edged historical significance in ancient Greece. On the one hand, she exposes vividly the vulnerability of women as pawns in a fundamentally masculine game of political and social chess. Yet on the other hand she also reveals the danger that women could pose even, or especially, to elite citizen men, when the latter's opponents could represent them in the uncomfortably public glare of a civic courtroom as in any way less than fully capable of controlling their womenfolk as "real" men should.

CHAPTER 13

ARISTOTLE

OF STAGIRA AND ATHENS

THE SCHOOL OF ATHENS
Raphael

Our word "school" derives ultimately from the ancient Greek word meaning "leisure." Only the leisured elites had the time and money to be able to afford to attend the sort of schools—of higher learning—that Plato and Aristotle established in Athens in the 4th century. Raphael's masterpiece is centered on these two giant thinkers, teacher and pupil, and by the gestures he attributes to them he seems to have wanted to distinguish their whole philosophical systems and outlooks too. Whereas the older Plato points up, heavenwards, to his ideal world of the perfect metaphysical Forms, Aristotle points down to indicate his earthier, more materialistically grounded approach to the good life for mankind. *(Bridgeman Art Library/Vatican Museums and Galleries)*

Aristotle is one of those people whose name seems to be an omen of their destiny. Aristoteles (the original Greek form) is a combination of *ariston,* "best," and *telos,* "end," and Aristotle was a teleological philosopher. That is, he believed that in nature, every living thing has built into it at conception and birth its predestined final end, its perfected form. For example, the "end" of an acorn is the fully mature oak tree. So, by extension, the "end" of all human social life and organization was for Aristotle the Greek *polis*. This reminds us that although Aristotle is probably best known today as a logician and political philosopher, he was at bottom a scientist, more particularly a botanist and zoologist. Yet for all his intellectual brilliance, alas, he personally did not come to the best of ends.

Aristotle's intellectual formation, output, and legacy were procured essentially through his experience in Athens, the "city hall of wisdom," as his teacher Plato once called it. But though a pupil of Plato's Academy from the age of seventeen (he was born in 384), and though in the mid-330s he founded his own institute of higher learning, the Lyceum, in a grove sacred to Apollo Lyceius at Athens (the site has recently been

201

ARISTOTLE

The Stagirite, so named for his home city of Stagira in northern Greece, was the original "Renaissance man." Aristotle covered, or pioneered, or systematized, virtually all the then-recognized branches of knowledge and learning. He founded the Lyceum institute in Athens, attracting pupils from as far away as Lesbos. His end, however, was less than happy, since he got tarred with the brush of being a Macedonian sympathizer because of his personal connections with the Macedonian court. (Le Louvre, Paris) uncovered), Aristotle was never an Athenian citizen, but only an Athenian resident alien. He was born in and retained the citizenship of his native Stagira or Stagirus in Chalcidice in northern Greece, which is why he is sometimes referred to as "the Stagirite." And he returned north temporarily in the later 340s, at the request of Philip II, king of neighboring Macedon, to tutor the young Alexander (later the Great). There was a personal as well as an intellectual reason for this invitation and acceptance: Aristotle's own father Nicomachus had been court physician to Philip's father Amyntas.

Aristotle thus embodies the key political shift that took place during his lifetime in the balance of power within the old Greek world. The Peloponnesian War had been fought between the southern Greek powers of Athens and Sparta and their allies, with the northern Greeks very much on the periphery of things most of the time. But by 336, when Philip II was assassinated while celebrating the wedding of Alexander's sister, Macedon had become the undisputed single great power of the Greek world. It was ultimately for his connections with Macedon—far too cozy in the eyes of Athenian patriots—that Aristotle was to suffer his premature death in 322.

In 367, however, when Aristotle made the journey south to sit at Plato's feet, Philip not only had not yet come to the throne of Macedon but was actually being held hostage in Thebes, which was then, under Epaminondas, at the apex of its influence. The 360s are sometimes referred to as the "hegemony" or "ascendancy" of Thebes. But, as we have seen, the Battle of Mantinea in 362 brought confusion and disturbance once more, and the divided Greek cities of central and southern mainland Greece were notoriously unable to unite sufficiently to resist the southwards expansion of Philip, which climaxed on the field of Chaeronea in Boeotia in 338. Thereafter, through what modern scholars call the League of

Corinth, Philip in effect had a stranglehold on the Aegean Greek world and deprived the Greek cities in his power of their cherished freedom and autonomy. Yet Aristotle never gave up his belief that the real essence, the true nature, of Greek politics lay in the individual city-state, the *polis*.

About three years after Chaeronea, Aristotle returned to Athens following a long sojourn away in northern Greece (in Macedonia, as just mentioned), the east Aegean (where he met his future pupil and successor Theophrastus on Sappho's island of Lesbos), and Asia Minor (where he married the ward of an intellectually-minded dynast called Hermeias). He shortly thereafter founded the Lyceum and quickly proved himself a master of research in more than one sense: both in carrying out researches himself into just about every field of scholarship then recognized, and in organizing and supervising the researches of his pupils, some of them collaborative. This all has a remarkably contemporary feel. So too does the way he and his pupils drew up the ancient equivalent of databases (entirely by hand, of course, and preserved on expensive papyrus). He created the first ever research library, which after his death passed eventually to the Ptolemies of Egypt and became the founding core of the great Library of Alexandria.

Aristotle's writings were often based on his lectures, and some of the preserved texts have a very oral quality to them. In antiquity all five hundred or so of his attributed "books" were divided into two main groups: the "exoteric" and the "esoteric"—that is, those designed to be read by a slightly wider general public outside the confines of his school, and those designed solely for the use of his pupils within the school. Unfortunately, in some ways, the thirty "books" that have survived to us are all "esoteric," composed for internal consumption, and therefore often written in allusive, elliptical style, sometimes, indeed, in lecture-note form. This does not help our understanding of them, which is difficult enough in light of their complex subject matter.

The ancient Greek word meaning inquiry or research was *historia*, from which we get our word "history," though we use that in its original sense only in the phrase "natural history." *Historia* may have been a term employed by the man who is probably to be seen as Aristotle's ultimate intellectual ancestor, Thales of Miletus, who flourished in the first half of the sixth century and was later included in various slightly varying lists of the "Seven Wise Men" of ancient Greece. It was certainly used by Herodotus, who in the preface refers to his work as the "exposition" of his "research" into Helleno-Barbarian and especially Helleno-Persian interaction and, ultimately, conflict. A character in Euripides praises the manifold blessings of research, and his younger contemporary Democritus (another northern Greek, from Abdera) was surely the most remarkable all-round researcher before Aristotle. Indeed, Aristotle recognized Democritus's stature by writing a commentary on his predecessor's atomistic theory (with which he disagreed), "theory" being another of our key Greek-derived terms, from *theoria,* meaning contemplation. In Aristotle's *Nicomachean Ethics* (so-called because the book was supposed to have been written for his son Nicomachus) he concludes by recommending *theoria* as the morally highest human goal, the supreme form of happiness, superior even to a life of active politics.

But before he researched and formulated his theory of politics he practiced natural science, admittedly without the possibility of using the experimental method in a way that we would consider adequate but including dissection where feasible and above all paying attention to the minutest and most accurate description of observable (to the naked eye—no microscopes) phenomena with a view to their classification, analysis, and generalizable interpretation. Two passages from his *Parts of Animals* have a wide application to Aristotle's work as a whole*:

> Every study and investigation, the humblest and noblest alike, seems to admit of two kinds of proficiency; one of which may be properly called educated knowledge of the subject, while the other is a kind of acquaintance with it. For an educated man should be able to form a fair judgment as to the goodness or badness of an exposition. To be educated is in fact to be able to do this; and the man of general education we take to be such. It will, however, of course be understood that we ascribe universal education only to one who in his own individual person is thus able to judge nearly all branches of knowledge, and not to one who has a like ability merely in some special subject...

> We proceed to treat of animals, without omitting, to the best of our ability, any member of the kingdom, however ignoble. For if some have no graces to charm the sense, yet nature, which fashioned them, gives amazing pleasure in their study to all who can trace links of causation, and are inclined to philosophy... We must not therefore recoil with childish aversion from the examination of the humbler animals...

There speaks and breathes the truly scientific spirit, the same sort of spirit of inquiry that animated all Aristotle's re-

---

* Translation from the Bollingen Series. See the "Suggested Reading" for details.

In the *Politics,* Aristotle specifically says that the women (wives, daughters) of the poor (adult male) citizens could not be restricted within the house but had to go out for necessary economic purposes. Running water in the home was not on offer in most of ancient Greece, so a visit to the public well was a daily chore for many Greek women, who no doubt entertained themselves at the same time by exchanging news of births, marriages and deaths. *(Museo Nazionale di Villa Giulia, Rome)*

searches into the human as well as the non-human worlds of nature. A like spirit had notably informed the medical observations of the doctors associated with the "Hippocratic" school of medicine named after the great fifth-century doctor Hippocrates from the island of Cos. One of these began his treatise *On the Sacred Disease* (epilepsy) by observing that, despite its name, and contrary to popular opinion, epilepsy was no more or less sacred than any other disease and equally susceptible to rational analysis and treatment. It was entirely fitting that Aristotle's father should have been a medical man.

A similar scientific concern for observation, classification, analysis, and generalization informs Aristotle's great work of political science and political theory, the *Politics*, which he composed towards the end of his life at around 330 or so. Not that he was the first to apply scientific method to politics, by any means. As early as Herodotus we find a passage, the so-called Persian Debate, which is premised on the brilliant discovery that all forms of human government must be species of just three genera: rule by one, rule by some, rule by all. Hence (to use Herodotus's own illustrations): monarchy (the rule of a hereditary autocrat), aristocracy (the rule of a few exceptionally virtuous and well-qualified men), and democracy (the rule of all the People by the People and for the People). Aristotle's *Politics* was from one point of view the working out of this insight to the furthest scientific degree within the given framework of the Greek *polis*.

For Aristotle the teleologist believed that, in his famous phrase, man was a "political animal" in the precise sense that humans were designed by their nature to realize their full self-expression through living the good life within, and only within, the framework of the self-governing Greek city-state or *polis*. The name for the free adult males who were granted full entitlement within the *polis* was *politai*, *polis*-persons or citizens;

and Aristotle defined the citizen as the man who shares in political judgment and rule. This permissive definition was, he admitted, most appropriate to the citizen of a democratic state. But Aristotle was not himself an ideological democrat. In this he was at one with almost all known classical Greek thinkers.

This intellectual hostility to democracy, which we have met most concretely in Socrates, may well surprise and dismay us today. But intellectuals were members of the ancient Greek social elite—wealthy, leisured, and well educated—whereas most ancient Greek citizens were not. The ancient Greek form of democracy—direct democracy, or government by mass meeting, as it's sometimes called—gave to those ordinary Greeks the kind of collective say in deciding their fate that we today can only wonder at or envy. To most ancient Greek elite intellectuals it seemed that the collective say of the masses was a form of dictatorship of the proletariat, exercised over—that is, against the interests of—themselves.

That is one reason why there is so little explicitly democratic political theory from ancient Greece, though Aristotle, again unlike Plato, does his best to be fair to democratic conceptions and ideals. His ideal, however, as expressed in the last two books of the *Politics*, was some sort of intellectually wise and morally virtuous aristocracy—a government by people rather like himself. But then most of us tend to fashion utopia in our own image.

The mundane historical reality in which Aristotle was then living was a very different matter. Greece, as we have seen, was from the early 330s in the grip of Macedon, an authoritarian kingdom. Alexander was extending that grip to Asia, to the former Persian empire. There was little scope left there for an Aristotelian utopia on the *polis* scale. Besides, Athens, the city in which Aristotle chose to live most of his adult life, was becoming a diehard enemy of Macedon, ready to risk all on a vi-

olent uprising against the suzerain of Greece in 323. That revolt, known as the Lamian War, attracted widespread support
but foundered completely on the rock of Macedonian military
and naval superiority. Alexander himself had died, but the
might of Macedon was easily sufficient to crush Athens. The
Macedonian powers-that-be decided they had had enough of
the Athenian democracy. They duly terminated it in 322.

Aristotle and Demosthenes, for their own different reasons,
found it expedient to leave Athens at this juncture. Demosthenes took his life on Calaureia, the modern island of Poros;
Aristotle ended his at Chalcis on the island of Euboea. He is reported to have said that he was committing suicide in order to
prevent the Athenians from sinning twice against philosophy,
a reference to the trial and death of Socrates.

If those were his famous last words, they were entirely appropriate to a not only brilliant but also decently humane man.
In his will, the terms of which are preserved, he left adequate
provision for his wife and family, including instructions to
manumit personal slaves. But his real legacy is his extraordinary intellectual output, unsurpassed in either range or overall
quality throughout antiquity.

CHAPTER 14

OLYMPIAS

OF EPIRUS AND MACEDON

ALEXANDRIA

Alexandria was the queen of Alexander the Great's city foundations, of which there were at least six and perhaps as many as twenty. Here it is represented on a late Antique mosaic map from Madaba. What the mapmaker could not show were the great Museum and Library founded by Alexander's immediate successor as ruler of Egypt, Ptolemy I, the founder of the line of which Cleopatra was the last representative. *(Archaeological Museum, Gerasa, Jordan)*

The Greek navy not long ago commissioned a rather unusual warship: not nuclear-powered but oar-powered, made predominantly not of metal but of wood. For this was a replica—or at least an intended replica—of an ancient Greek trireme warship, designed by a British naval architect following the instructions of a British classical scholar. All ships must of course have a name and, by convention, a female name. This new recruit was duly baptized "Olympias," after the mother of Alexander the Great.

Now, one might well have thought that, if the name of a famous ancient Greek woman with naval associations was required, the name of Artemisia might more readily have sprung to mind, though there was of course the minor obstacle that she had performed her naval feats on the wrong, anti-Greek side. Still, Olympias, a Greek from Epirus married to a king of Macedon, neither of them regions with powerful naval traditions in her day, was hardly the most obvious choice. Presumably, therefore, current political preoccupations had something to do with it. There is, nevertheless, something rather appealing about the thought of a revived Olympias again riding, or rather cutting through, the ocean wave. The original was certainly one of the most go-getting and colorful of all ancient Greeks who left their indelible impress on the historical record.

Alexander, Olympias's first-born, clearly found his mother difficult. He is reported to have once quipped that she charged him a high rent for the nine months she had housed him in her womb. Philip, too—her husband, Philip II of Macedon— found her a hot property. She was not his first wife nor his last; in all he amassed seven in the course of some twenty years, several of them concurrently. One ancient biographer remarked that he fought his wars by marriages, that is, he made diplomatic marriages in order to complement his warmaking with programmatic lovemaking. But Olympias was, thanks not least to her own machinations, the senior wife, though that was a position she felt called upon to defend constantly by all available means.

Romantic contemporaries liked to imagine that the marriage of Philip and Olympias was a love-match. The couple had first met, so it was rumored, while separately taking part in the secret mystery-rites held on the northern Aegean island of Samothrace. The less exciting reality is surely that, like the other six, this was the outcome of diplomatic matchmaking. At any rate, they don't seem to have been matched temperamentally. Olympias was the more passionate and mystic, Philip the more hardheaded and pragmatic. Alexander, born in 356, appears to have suffered as a child, caught between his warring parents. Olympias may even have told her son that Philip was not really his father. In later years, the no less mystic Alexander liked to put it about that his real as opposed to "so-called" father was a god.

On one day in the summer of 356 Philip allegedly received three messages. His premier general, Parmenion, had won a key victory against a particularly troublesome neighboring non-Greek people, a racehorse of his had gained a victory in the Olympic Games, and Olympias had given birth to the son whom he called Alexander (meaning "defender of men," a traditional Macedonian royal name). The good news for Philip did not end there. The most powerful Greek states, including some who were his declared enemies, were embroiled in two serious wars, the Social War (involving Athens and her naval alliance) and the Sacred War (for control of the body that administered the lucrative shrine of Delphi), thereby weakening themselves to Macedon's and his own potential profit. But for Olympias the struggle for power and influence had only just begun.

She could not prevent Philip marrying other women, including non-Greek women, and having children with them (the famous, recently excavated "Tomb of Philip" at modern Vergina (ancient Aegae), contained besides the male skeleton and appropriate accoutrements, a female skeleton accompanied by non-Greek military paraphernalia, reasonably identified as his penultimate, Scythian wife.) But she could try to ensure that these other wives were subordinate to her and that their male offspring were all behind Alexander in the line for succession to the Macedonian throne.

The court at Pella, the capital of Macedon, thus came to have a decidedly oriental feel to it; at any rate, that is how it would have appeared to an outside Greek observer such as Herodotus. In fact, in terms of its dynastic politics it not only resembled a contemporary oriental court but also foreshadowed the typical royal court of the post-Alexander Hellenistic Greek world (traditionally dated 323–30 B.C.E.). Greek cities, of course, remained in existence and in some ways flourished during that era, but they were almost all immediately subject to one or another Hellenistic territorial monarch who lived in a palace surrounded by courtiers. Mothers and aunts of actual and potential rulers exercised an unusually powerful influence in these, for Greeks, new political surroundings.

Olympias, it seems, though Greek by birth, was well ahead of the game and fully exploited these alien dynamics to her best advantage. It helped, of course, that she was the daughter of a hereditary ruler, Neoptolemus, who was king of the Molossian people. These Greeks lived in Epirus in the north-west at the very edge of the pale of Greek civilization. Like other frontier Greeks—in Cyprus and Sicily, for instance—the city-state form had not sunk roots as deep as those of the old Greek heartland, and political conditions demanded the existence of a strong, centralized military executive that was most easily satisfied by having a hereditary monarchy.

Olympias thus passed from the hands of one king to another, but Philip was a very different proposition from Neoptolemus. He was a master diplomat as well as a more than competent general, with the sense to realize that before he could advance his ambitions on a wider front he must first unify Macedon itself. This he did by a combination of threats and blandishments, bribes and concessions, securing the loyalty of the "barons" of upper—that is, western—Macedon, among whom was Philip's premier general throughout his reign, Parmenion. Alexander was to inherit him from Philip for his Asiatic campaign—and to have him murdered.

Olympias does not seem to have had a problem with Parmenion. But she did with others of Philip's noble Macedonian henchman, especially Attalus and Antipater. In 337 Philip married wife number seven, Attalus' niece and the first wife he had taken from the blue-blooded, upper-class Macedonian nobility. Attalus, Olympias inferred, had his eyes on the long-term succession to Philip, who was then only forty-five years old, with a view to diverting it from her bloodline. Her suspicion seemed only confirmed when at the wedding ceremony

Attalus prayed conspicuously that the couple might produce a legitimate Macedonian heir. Alexander behaved badly, and both he and his mother judged it prudent to distance themselves from Pella for a time, Olympias withdrawing to her family home in Epirus.

The withdrawal seems to have been fruitful. The following year her daughter with Philip, Alexander's full sister Cleopatra, was married to Olympias's brother: the links between Pella and Molossia, and the prospects for Alexander's succession, seemed more secure again. But at the wedding ceremony for Cleopatra and Olympias's brother, held at Aegae, Philip was assassinated. The finger of suspicion was pointed at Alexander, not implausibly. He, though only twenty years old, probably had the most to gain from his father's removal from the scene then, and he certainly behaved in a way that suggested he had something to hide. What that something may have been, so it was rumored at the time and so it has been believed in some recent scholarship, was that the order for the assassination had been given, not by Alexander, but by Olympias, on his, and so her own, behalf.

That, of course, can never be proved, but the future course of Olympias's bloodstained career does little or nothing to squash the suspicion. Alexander was duly acclaimed king by the Macedonian army according to local custom, and in 334 he set off for his greatest adventure, the conquest of the Persian Empire, never to return to Macedonian soil. We have already mentioned his apparent distancing of himself from Philip's merely mortal paternity. Olympias would not necessarily have objected to that. On the other hand, we have also noticed Alexander's complaint that Olympias made life difficult for him. One reason might have been her personal conduct. Women in Greece were thought to be more prone to indulge themselves in ecstatic or mystic religious ritual than men.

Olympias's continued devotion to Orphic and Dionysiac cults seems tailormade to bolster such suppositions. Another reason was presumably her continued political lobbying—or gross interference—on behalf of what she considered Alexander's and her best interests.

At any rate, she had a serious falling out with the man Alexander had left behind as regent of Macedon, Antipater. By the end of 331 she had returned again to her native Epirus, and there she remained until 317. By then, however, Alexander had died (in 323), and the prolonged funeral games to decide the succession to his hugely inflated empire had been under way for half a dozen years. (They were not to be completed until 301.) Olympias weighed in with both military force and vicarious murder of royal rivals, combined with symbolic appeal to the memory of her late husband and son, in order, apparently, to make herself the power not merely behind but actually on the Macedonian throne. The Macedonian assembly—that is, in effect, the main Macedonian army—condemned her to death, and in 316 she was killed by relatives of her victims. Her son fared, on the whole, rather better.

CHAPTER 15

ALEXANDER

OF MACEDON

On this mosaic from Pompeii, probably based on a Hellenistic painting, Alexander is shown confronting Darius III at the Battle of Issos in 333 B.C.E., the second of the three decisive pitched battles whereby he wrested the Persian empire for himself and his successors. *(Museo Archeologico Nazionale, Naples)*

For reconstructing the life and motivational mainsprings of Alexander the Great, there are lots of sources, but none or almost none are both contemporary and reliable. In Alexander's case this outcome is a little paradoxical. He had taken unusually many and careful measures to ensure that remembrance of his feats was available as far and as widely as possible. He had, for example, appointed an official historian, a relative of his old tutor Aristotle, as chronicler of his expedition against the Persian empire. Then there were several contemporaries, some intimates of his, who we know took up the stylus to record their version of events and especially, of course, their contribution to what Homer and Herodotus would have called "the wondrous deeds of men."

But the official chronicler was executed on Alexander's orders, and none of the contemporary writings has survived intact. What evidence we do have, apart from the contemporary archaeological data and the relatively few contemporary documents, are several narratives composed many centuries later by authors at the mercy of their sources, and a biography by Plutarch, who starts it discouragingly by saying that his pur-

221

pose is to write not history but biography. Nevertheless, the main lineaments of Alexander's extraordinary, unprecedented, and unparalleled career as conqueror between 336 and 323 are broadly agreed, and there are enough clues to his inner personality to make a stab at evaluating it. Still, it is salutary to recall at the outset that we probably all create the Alexander of our dreams; that is, we re-create him, to some extent, in our own relatively feeble images.

He came to the throne of Macedon, and so acceded to the position of most powerful ruler in the east Mediterranean Greek world, in 336, at the age of twenty. The circumstances were, to put it gently, murky, following his father Philip's assassination. But Alexander knew the way to reassure the old Macedonian nobility and the army that he was the right man for the job: a victorious military campaign. So he plunged first southwards to central Greece, where there was reported disaffection with Macedonian suzerainty, to assume his inheritance as leader of the League of Corinth and prospective leader of the crusade against the Persian Empire.

The following year he marched off in the opposite direction, northwards as far as the Danube, as if intending to make that his northern frontier. These were not his first taste of military command: that he had had already in 340 at the age of sixteen. But they were commands that required more than just military acumen. Alexander showed that he also had a shrewd political head on his young shoulders, not least in 335, when once again disaffection flared within the League of Corinth. This time his reaction was utterly ruthless. He ordered that Thebes be totally destroyed, razed to the ground, with the exception of its religious structures (to conciliate the gods) and the house in which Pindar had once lived (this last gesture was made to establish his credentials as a sensitive exponent of Greek culture on the eve of his

ALEXANDER

Alexander is said to have commissioned only one official sculptor, Lysippus, who depicted Alexander in his favored leonine pose. Deep beneath the exterior ran a current of yearning for ever further places or ever greater deeds. Some images of Alexander seem to capture this quintessential *pothos* of his. *(lower Agora, Pergamon, Turkey)*

One of Alexander's satraps (viceroys), a non-Greek, had himself buried at Sidon in a magnificent sarcophagus depicting the exploits of his great patron. Alexander had first come to general notice as commander of the elite Companion Cavalry of Macedon at the Battle of Chaeronea in 338. It was fitting that he should have been represented here in characteristic mounted attitude. *(Archaeological Museum, Istanbul)*

anti-barbarian campaign of vengeance for the destruction wreaked by Xerxes in 480–479, when Thebes had been on the Persian side).

In 334, finally, he was ready to take over in person in Asia from Parmenion, whom Philip had sent on ahead shortly before he was assassinated. In a series of three set-piece battles of ascending difficulty and importance (the Granicus River in 334, Issus in 333, and Gaugamela in Assyria in 331), he overcame the more numerous but also more heterogeneous and less than fanatically loyal forces at the disposal of King Darius III. He also, in the meanwhile, carried out his paradoxical objective of defeating the Persian fleet by land—that is, by capturing its main bases such as (most spectacularly) Tyre. And in 332, moreover, having captured Egypt, he set the seal on his new acquisition by laying the foundations of what was to become the greatest capital of the Hellenistic Greek world, Alexandria, named, of course, after himself.

Even before the final defeat of Darius at Gaugamela, Alexander had proclaimed that he, not Darius, was the legitimate ruler of the Persian empire. An odd claim, on the face of it, but the point was to prepare the old Persian nobility and, no less important, the old Macedonian nobility, for his transformation into an unprecedented mixture of a Graeco-Macedonian and oriental monarch. He began to wear a modified version of Persian regalia. He reappointed noble Persians to their rule over formerly Persian satrapies, now Macedonian provinces. He even tried to amalgamate his Macedonian and his Persian courts, by way of the symbolic ritual of *proskunesis* or obeisance (the kowtow).

All this aroused disquiet or worse among his Macedonians, most ominously among the high military command. Alexander, as we have seen, not only inherited Parmenion from Philip as his premier general but also kept him on in that position for several years after his own assumption of the monarchy. Indeed, he somehow acquiesced in—perhaps he felt he had no choice, perhaps he felt it did not constitute a threat—the presence among the highest military command of not only Parmenion himself but also his son Philotas (commander of the elite Companion Cavalry) and other of Parmenion's relatives by birth or marriage, together with a number of their known close associates and supporters. But in 330, following the symbolic conclusion of the Hellenic campaign of revenge (with the torching of the Persian royal palace at Persepolis, the old empire's ceremonial capital), Alexander decided the time had come to strike out for his independence—by striking down the Parmenion circle.

Philotas was executed on grounds of alleged treachery. His father was simply murdered as a security risk. Command structures were altered, and the ensuing posts of high command were assigned to new, totally safe, pro-Alexander hands. Still, the opposition persisted, and, indeed, grew. Perhaps he did not mean to murder a senior commander and boyhood friend at Samarcand in 328—he was, after all, blind drunk at the time. But that did nothing to allay the suspicion that Alexander's orientalism was verging on the despotic. In 327 his Greek official historian, Callisthenes, was even prepared to openly oppose yet another attempt of Alexander's to introduce the Persian custom of obeisance as standard for Macedonians and Greeks as well as orientals. A plot was then opportunely uncovered among the Royal Pages, the king's own special entourage of young nobles and prospective courtiers, and amid the recriminations that followed, Callisthenes was denounced and executed.

All this was against the background of probably the toughest campaigning in all the ten years of his campaign, during which Alexander's troops were confronted by nationalist guerrillas in the terrain of what is today roughly Afghanistan. Still

Alexander pressed on relentlessly eastwards, over the Hindu Kush into what is now Pakistan. Why so far? What was impelling him? His troops suspected mere megalomania, a suspicion that received some confirmation from the frenzied lengths to which Alexander would drive them when opposed or (as he saw it) crossed. Conditions were now such as the Macedonians and the relatively few Greek troops left had never experienced—huge rivers, elephants, monsoon rains.

At the river Hyphasis (modern Beas) they at last mutinied. Alexander had no choice but to agree to proceed no further. Instead he turned south and conducted what can only be called a campaign of blood towards the Indus delta. Not that Alexander spared himself. He was nearly killed leading the assault on one Indian town and he shared the privations of his ordinary troops on their long forced march back along the Persian gulf to Persia. But what was it all for? To satisfy some deep personal longing or lust, perhaps connected with his vision of his divine descent and predestined future, or merely to further his own power and glory?

On his return to civilization at the heart of the old Persian Empire in 325 he found the administration of many parts of his new empire in serious disarray. Allegations of treachery were freely bandied about, several satraps were now executed, and some old personal scores were settled. But still there was little sign that Alexander himself intended to settle—that is, to settle down. His thoughts turned once again to the problem of his native Macedon and the mainland of Greece, so far away across the water. His thoughts were not entirely constructive, as the Greek cities saw it. For in 324 he ordered them to receive back their exiles, wherever they were or however they had come to be such. Not only was this, formally, an illegal breach of the League of Corinth agreement, but it also caused severe practical chaos.

An order to accord him divine honors, if he did indeed issue such an order, will not have helped matters either. Alexander was not the first Greek to receive divine honors in his lifetime, but the precedents were very few and of course, inevitably, inexact. Greek envoys nevertheless did come to salute him in Babylon in 323, wearing ceremonial wreaths to indicate that they were performing an act of religious homage, but, as our best surviving source (Arrian) wryly puts it, "his end was near." That is, Alexander was no immortal god. And in fact he died in June 323 in Babylon, probably not, as was rumored, of poison but rather of an infection that took hold of a constitution weakened by the exceptional stress to which he had subjected it over many years, not least through a prodigious intake of alcohol.

What then, to ask the question again, did drive Alexander? What, to change the metaphor, really made him tick? One word that recurs in the sources in connection with some of his more fantastic projects is *pothos*, meaning an unusually powerful longing for some unusually difficult goal. This fits well with his devotion to Homer and the ideal of such heroes as Achilles and Patroclus who continually strove to be first and among the best. Indeed, having run out of mortal men to rival it seems as though Alexander set himself to emulate heroes (Heracles) and even gods (Dionysus), perhaps because he considered that nothing less than that was owed to his superhuman origins.

A key episode in this connection is a visit, really a side-trip, he undertook to Siwah in the western desert far beyond the Nile delta in 332, when the still incomplete campaign against Darius should have occupied his full attention. Instead, he braved horrendous conditions to visit the oracular shrine of Ammon, to ask Ammon (the Libyan version of the Egyptian Amun, identified by Greeks as equivalent to their Zeus) something about his *genesis*, that is, his birth or conception. Various conflicting stories emerged as to what exactly Alexander had asked, and what Ammon, through his priest, had replied. But it is certain that Alexander himself did later refer important actions of his back to what he had claimed he learned and been instructed at Siwah. So perhaps here lies an important part of what turned Alexander into something more than just a Macedonian military conqueror.

His empire as such perished with him, as we have seen. No one man was big enough to inherit and control the lot. But his legacy of Hellenism, so far from perishing in 323, went on to flourish in all sorts of unexpected corners and in all sorts of unpredictable ways. That the New Testament was written in Greek, for example, although it was written for Palestinian Jews whose first language was Aramaic, is just one example of this legacy of Alexander.

Another is the Museum and Library at Alexandria, founded by Alexander's boyhood friend Ptolemy, who had hijacked Alexander's corpse as it was en route for burial in Macedon and had it entombed magnificently at Alexandria as the legitimating talisman of his rule. Through Alexandrian scholarship the literary heritage of old Greece was preserved and transmitted, first to the conquering Romans and then to their successors, the Byzantines, and ultimately, via the Renaissance of classical scholarship, to us.

EPILOGUE

Shakespeare's Hamlet mused irreverently on the possible fate of Alexander's remains as the mud that might be used to caulk a humble beer-barrel. But that is just the way we ordinary mortals typically do seek to render comprehensible extraordinary ones like Alexander—by bringing them down to our own sordid level.

It is to be hoped that, though I have not sought to disguise the many faults of the Greeks, I have nevertheless managed to do justice to their often extraordinary and still potent achievements. True, by our standards—or the ideal standards of some of us, perhaps—their culture was often bigoted and narrowminded: they were sexist, for example, and they practiced the enslavement of human beings. But they also produced breathtakingly original and permanently influential works of visual and written art to which even our postmodern, electronic age pays homage in countless and usually unrecognized ways.

Above all, though, I personally respect the Greeks for having invented the idea of criticism (*kritikos* was the adjective of *krites*, the noun meaning a judge), and above all self-criticism. They would, most of them, probably have liked to have been eternally conservative, and many often were traditionally-minded to an extreme degree. But the mark of a progressive culture as a whole is whether it can see beyond tradition; indeed, whether it can subject the very idea of tradition to an internal critique. That the Greeks succeeded in doing beyond all other known peoples before or since.

Let me end with a couple of illustrations that will, I hope, bring home my point. First, readers might perhaps begin by calling to their minds a recent major national or international conflict that involved considerations of personal and political identity and ideology rather than mere economic self-interest, say the Vietnam War or the Gulf War, or, more recently, the bombing of Kosovo. Next I would ask them to transport themselves back in their imagination to Athens in late winter/early spring 415 B.C.E., to the theater of Dionysus, where a performance of Euripides' new tragedy *The Trojan Women* is being performed. The plot is traditional, as traditional as could be—it is lifted, after all, directly from Homer's *Iliad*. But the treatment is as untraditional, as contemporary, and as self-critical as could be.

Euripides invites his largely (exclusively?) male and Athenian audience of fifteen thousand or so to imagine what it would be like to be women about to be carted off into slavery in a foreign land and thrust into the beds of their conquerors, the men who have killed their own husbands and children. Nor are these ordinary, let alone despicable women, but noble women with minds and tongues of their own.

That in itself would have been startling or shocking enough. But the context added a further, perhaps even more unsettling, dimension. Immediately before this performance of the mythical plot about the women of Troy, some of the members of the audience had been involved, admittedly on a much smaller scale, in doing pretty much what their mythical ancestors had been doing at and to Troy. What is more, they had done it to a Greek, not a barbarian, city. In the winter of 416–415, the Athenians, aided by some allies, had killed all the adult male citizens of the Aegean island-city of Melos that they could get hold of, and had sold the women and children into slavery.

We do not know, directly, what impact Euripides' play had. But we do, I believe, get an indirect reflection of it in the very different genre of history as written by Thucydides. In terms of affecting the course of the Peloponnesian War, the Melos massacre was pretty small beer. In any case, the Melians were pro-Spartan and oligarchs, and so, by the laws of war, got what was coming to them. Yet Thucydides did not see things quite that way. He selected this episode as the moment for a profound reflection on the implications of imperialism—not just Athenian imperialism, but all imperialism. The Melian Dialogue, as it is called, can still be read with profit as a profound meditation on the morality—the immorality, the amorality—of grossly disproportionate inter-state power-relations. That, surely, is what we mean by classical.

It is also a crucial part of what Plato's Socrates meant when he declared famously in the *Apology* (a version of his defense speech when on trial for his life for impiety in 399 B.C.E.) that "the unexamined life is not worth living." In that sense, but only in that sense, we may legitimately agree with Shelley's equally famous claim that "We are all Greeks." For we are emphatically *not* ancient Greeks in several utterly basic respects: we do not keep slaves, let alone base our civilization on the exploitation of slave labor, nor do we enshrine in law a second-class status for women out of the conviction that women, all women, are "naturally" inferior to all men. On the other hand, we *are* still all Greeks today in that we believe fundamentally in what the Greeks called *logos*: the application of logic and rationality through processes of social debate and internal self-criticism, and the overriding value of reason, argument, and reckoning delivered either in speech or in writing. Perhaps the classic illustration is the invention of democracy attributed to one of the most intriguing of our fifteen subjects, Cleisthenes of Athens.

In summary, we might conclude by paraphrasing the opening of the Gospel of St. John, whose author was himself deliberately giving an old thought a new Christian spin: in the beginning of our own civilization and culture was ancient Greek Logos.

SUGGESTIONS FOR FURTHER READING

GENERAL

Sue Blundell, *Women in Ancient Greece* (Cambridge, MA: Harvard University Press & London: British Museum Press, 1995).

Paul Cartledge, *The Greeks: A Portrait of Self and Others* (Oxford: Oxford University Press, 1997).

Paul Cartledge (ed.), *The Cambridge Illustrated History of Ancient Greece* (Cambridge & New York: Cambridge University Press, 1998).

Elaine Fantham et al., *Women in the Classical World* (New York: O.U.P., 1994).

Charles Freeman, *The Greek Achievement* (NY: Viking and London: Penguin, 1999).

Robert Garland, *Daily Life of the Ancient Greeks* (Westport, CT & London: Greenwood Press, 1998).

Peter Jones et al., *The World of Athens* (Cambridge: C.U.P., 1984).

Mary Lefkowitz & Maureen B. Fant, *Women's Life in Greece & Rome*, 2nd ed. (Baltimore: Johns Hopkins U.P. & London: Duckworth, 1982).

Neville Morley, *Writing Ancient History* (London: Duckworth, 1999).

Sarah Pomeroy et al., *Ancient Greece. A Political, Social, and Cultural History* (New York: O.U.P., 1998).

HOMER

Numerous translations of both the *Iliad* and the *Odyssey* exist in both verse and prose. The most successful modern verse renderings are perhaps those of either Robert Fitzgerald or Robert Fagles; some scholars, however, prefer those of Richmond Lattimore for their greater literal fidelity. The most successful, commercially, of all modern renderings are the prose versions of E.V. Rieu, of which the *Odyssey* has been reissued in an edition revised by his son and introduced by Peter Jones (Penguin Books). But for me, at any rate, any prose translation, however excellent on its own terms, cannot fail to denature the poetic quintessence of the originals.

Secondary literature:

The Fagles translations come with excellent introductions by Bernard Knox.

See also:

C. Emlyn-Jones (ed.), *Homer: Readings and Images* (Milton Keynes: Open University, 1992).

Jasper Griffin, *Homer* ("Past Masters" series, Oxford: O.U.P., 1980).

For the Homeric tradition:

G. Steiner (ed.), *Homer in English* (London: Penguin, 1996).

W.B. Stanford, *The Ulysses Theme* 2nd ed. (Oxford: Blackwell, 1968).

SAPPHO

Sappho: Poems & Fragments, translated by Josephine Balmer (London: Brilliance Books ["a lesbian and gay press"], 1984).

These genuinely poetic renditions are incorporated in Balmer's also excellent *Classical Women Poets* (Newcastle: Bloodaxe, 1996).

Critical studies include:

Page duBois, *Sappho is Burning* (Chicago: University of Chicago Press, 1995).

Jane McIntosh Snyder, *Sappho* ("Lives of Notable Gay Men and Lesbians" series) (NY & Philadelphia: Chelsea House Publishers, 1995).

Margaret Williamson, *Sappho's Immortal Daughters* (Cambridge, MA & London: Harvard University Press, 1995).

CLEISTHENES

Esp. *Herodotus* 5.66, 69, 72-3; 6.131 (trs. R. Waterfield, Oxford World Classics, 1998).

Mogens H. Hansen, *The Athenian Democracy in the Age of Demosthenes* rev. edition (London: Bristol Classical Press & Duckworth, 1999).

Pierre Lévêque and Pierre Vidal-Naquet, *Cleisthenes the Athenian* (Atlantic Highlands, NJ: Humanities Press, 1996).

ARTEMISIA

Herodotus Book 7 ch. 99; 8 chs 68, 87, 101-3.

A.R. Burn, *Persia and the Greeks* (London: Duckworth, 1984).

J.M. Cook, *The Persian Empire* (London: Dent, 1983).

PERICLES

Plutarch, *Life of Pericles* [best read in the Oxford World's Classics edition: Plutarch, *Greek Lives*, translated by Robin Waterfield with notes by Philip Stadter (Oxford & NY: O.U.P., 1998). This selection also contains Plutarch's important *Themistocles*].

Anthony Podlecki, *Perikles and His Circle* (London & New York: Routledge, 1998).

ASPASIA

Aristophanes, *Acharnians* 526-9; Plato *Menexenus*; Plutarch *Pericles* 24-5, 30, 32.

Madeleine M. Henry, *Prisoner of History: Aspasia of Miletus and Her Biographical Tradition* (New York: O.U.P., 1995).

SOCRATES

Plato, *Apology*; Xenophon, *Apology* (both available in good Penguin Classics editions).

Paul Cartledge, *Aristophanes and His Theatre of the Absurd* rev. ed. (Bristol & London: Bristol Classical Press/Duckworth, 1999).

M.I. Finley, "Socrates and Athens," *Aspects of Antiquity* rev. ed. (London: Penguin, 1977).

Alexander Nehamas, *The Art of Living: Socratic Reflections from Plato to Foucault* (California & London: University of California Press, 1998).

I.F. Stone, *The Trial of Socrates* (London: Jonathan Cape, 1988).

Gregory Vlastos, *Socrates: Ironist and Moral Philosopher* (Cambridge: Cambridge University Press, 1991).

Vlastos, *Socratic Studies*, ed. M. Burnyeat (Cambridge: Cambridge University Press, 1994).

CYNISCA

Xenophon, "Spartan society" (in Greek, *Lakedaimonion Politeia*) is available in translation either in the Loeb Classical Library series' Xenophon, *Scripta Minora* (which also contains the *Agesilaus*) or in R. Talbert, *Plutarch on Sparta* (Penguin Books, 1988).

There is also a much later biography of Agesilaus, dependent on Xenophon's, by Plutarch (c. c.e. 100), translated either in the Penguin volume by Ian Kilvert and Guy Griffith, Plutarch, *The Age of Alexander* or in Robin Waterfield & Philip Stadter *Plutarch: Greek Lives* (Oxford World Classics: Oxford, 1998).

Cynisca's inscription was included in a later collection of epigrams called *The Palatine Anthology* Book 13, no. 16; it is translated (slightly differently) by Peter Levi in his Penguin translation of *Pausanias: Guide to Greece* vol 2: *Southern Greece* (1971), p. 286.

Paul Cartledge, *Agesilaos and the Crisis of Sparta* (London: Duckworth & Baltimore: Johns Hopkins University Press, 1987).

Paul Cartledge, "The Greek Religious Festivals" in P. Easterling and J.V. Muir (eds.), R*eligion and Society in Ancient Greece* (Cambridge: Cambridge University Press, 1985).

Mark Golden, *Sport and Society in Ancient Greece* (Cambridge: Cambridge University Press, 1998).

EPAMINONDAS

Plutarch's life of Epaminondas is unfortunately lost, but his *Pelopidas* is extant: this appears in translation in the same Penguin collection as his *Agesilaus* cited above (see Chapter 8). The other main ancient source for his life and times is also late: Diodorus of Sicily, *Library of Greece* (c. 60–30 B.C.E.) esp. Book 15 (translated in the Loeb Classical Library series).

Epaminondas's epitaph is to be found in Peter Levi's Penguin translation of *Pausanias: Guide to Greece* vol 1: *Central Greece* (1971), p. 339.

There is no recent biography in English of Epaminondas. See:

John Buckler, *The Theban Hegemony* (Cambridge, MA: Harvard University Press, 1980).

Paul Cartledge, *Agesilaos* [as above, Chapter 8].

Victor Davis Hanson, *The Soul of Battle. From Ancient Times to the Present Day: How Three Great Liberators Vanquished Tyranny* (N.Y.: The Free Press, 1999) Part I "Yeomen of Thebes: Epaminondas's Descent into the Peloponnese."

Astonishingly, our hero was omitted from the recent German collection *Grosse Gestalten der griechischen Antike. 58 historische Portraits von Homer bis Kleopatra*, ed. K. Brodersen (Munich: Beck, 1999) ["Great Figures of Ancient Greece. 58 Historical Portraits from Homer to Cleopatra"].

DIOTIMA

Plato, *Symposium* 201–212 (speech and dialogue reported by Socrates): Numerous translations of the *Symposium* are available.

The following have their very different merits:

P.B. Shelley, "A Discourse on the Manners of the Ancient Greeks Relative to Love" in Richard Holmes (ed.), *Shelley on Love. An Anthology* (London: Anvil Press Poetry, 1980).

Tom Griffith, *Plato: Symposium* (London: Collins Harvill, 1989).

Alexander Nehamas & Paul Woodruff, *Plato: Symposium* (Indianapolis: Hackett).

H.A. Mason, *Fine Talk at Agathon's. A Version of Plato's Symposium* (Cambridge: *Cambridge Quarterly* Publications, 1992).

Robin Waterfield, *Plato: Symposium* (Oxford & NY: Oxford University Press, 1994).

The best commentary, but without a complete translation, is that of K.J. Dover (Cambridge: C.U.P. 1980 and repr.).

David M. Halperin, "Why is Diotima a woman?" in his *One Hundred Years of Homosexuality and Other Essays on Greek Love* (NY & London: Routledge, 1990).

PASION

Isocrates Speech 17. Demosthenes Speeches 36, 45, 46 are all available in the Loeb Classical Library series.

Edward Cohen, *Athenian Economy and Society: A Banking Perspective* (Princeton: Princeton University Press, 1992).

Nick Fisher, *Slavery in Classical Greece* (London: Bristol Classical Press/Duckworth, 1993).

Yvon Garlan, *Slavery in Ancient Greece* (Ithaca, NY: Cornell University Press, 1988).

T.R. Glover, "The House of Pasion" in *From Pericles to Philip* (London: Methuen, 1917), 302–336.

Paul Millett, *Lending and Borrowing in Ancient Athens* (Cambridge: C.U.P., 1991).

Jeremy Trevett, *Apollodorus the Son of Pasion* (Oxford: O.U.P., 1992).

NEAERA

As for Chapter 11, but add: Demosthenes 49, 50, 52, 53 (Apollodorus), and especially 59 "against Neaera."

A useful edition of the whole speech with translation is C. Carey, *Apollodorus Against Neaira [Demosthenes] 59* (Warminster: Aris & Phillips, 1992).

For translated extracts, and a useful discussion of Athenian society as a whole: Nick Fisher, *Social Values in Classical Athens* (London: Dent & Toronto: Hakkert, 1976).

ARISTOTLE

The most convenient and authoritative translations of all Aristotle's surviving works are in the 2-volume Bollingen Series edition, ed. Jonathan Barnes, (Princeton: Princeton University Press, 1984).

They are all included also in the Loeb Classical Library series. Individual philosophical works, esp. the *Nicomachean Ethics* and *Politics*, are available in Penguin Classics.

Science and other intellectual activity before Aristotle:

Paul Cartledge, *Democritus and Atomistic Politics* ("Great Philosophers" series) (London: Orion, 1998).

Terence Irwin, *Classical Thought* (Oxford: O.U.P., 1989).

Plato:

Richard Kraut (ed.), *The Cambridge Companion to Plato* (Cambridge: C.U.P., 1993).

Richard Rutherford, *The Art of Plato* (London: Duckworth, 1995).

Aristotle in the round:

Jonathan Barnes, *Aristotle* (Oxford: O.U.P., 1982).

Jonathan Barnes (ed.), *The Cambridge Companion to Aristotle* (Cambridge: C.U.P., 1995).

Geoffrey Lloyd, *Aristotle: The Growth of His Thought* (Cambridge: C.U.P., 1968).

OLYMPIAS

See next Chapter.

ALEXANDER

The best of an unsatisfactory bunch of extant ancient narratives is Arrian, *Anabasis* ("March Up Country"): good translations available both in the Loeb Classical Library series (P.A. Brunt, 1976–1983) and in Penguin Classics (A. de Sélincourt and J.R. Hamilton, 1971).

Plutarch's *Life of Alexander* is translated in I. Scott-Kilvert and G.T. Griffith, *The Age of Alexander* (Penguin Classics, 1971).

Brian Bosworth, *Conquest and Empire: The Reign of Alexander the Great* (Cambridge: C.U.P., 1988; "Canto" series repr. 1994).

Pierre Briant, *Alexander the Great* (London: Thames & Hudson, 1996 [French original 1987]).

Robin Lane Fox, *The Search for Alexander* (NY: Viking, 1980).

Ulrich Wilcken, *Alexander the Great,* ed. E.N. Borza (NY: Norton, 1967 [German original 1932]).

Mary Renault's Alexander Trilogy of historical novels (*Fire From Heaven*; *The Persian Boy*; and *Funeral Games*; repr. in 1 vol. Penguin Books) is infinitely superior to her avowedly non-fictional *The Nature of Alexander* (London: Allen Lane, 1975).

INDEX

ART CREDITS

ABOUT THE AUTHOR

PAUL CARTLEDGE is Professor of Greek History at the University of Cambridge, and Fellow and Director of Studies in Classics at Clare College, Cambridge. Over the course of his distinguished career he has written and edited numerous books on the ancient Greek world which are notable for their accessibility to the lay reader as well as being stimulating to the professional scholar. His publications include such works as the *Cambridge Illustrated History of Greece* and *The Greeks: A Portrait of Self and Others.*